The
Corncrake's
Welcome

Memoirs of a Northern Irish Diplomat

William D. Hanna

Troubador Publishing Ltd
Unit E2 Airfield Business Park,
Harrison Road, Market Harborough,
Leicestershire LE16 7UL
Tel: 0116 279 2299
Email: books@troubador.co.uk
Web: www.troubador.co.uk/matador

ISBN 978-1-80514-177-8

British Library Cataloguing in Publication Data.
A catalogue record for this book is available from the British Library.

Printed and bound in Great Britain by 4edge Limited
Typeset in 12pt Minion Pro by Troubador Publishing Ltd, Leicester, UK

Matador is an imprint of Troubador Publishing Ltd

For Luisa, David and Emilia:

"So walk with me now to the last field on the farm"

From 'The Last Field' by Michael Longley

Contents

Prologue   ix

Part 1: My Father's Story 1921–1936   **1**
The Sky Ablaze   3
Covenanters   10
The Corncrake's Welcome   14
Ballybradden   18
Wireless   22
A Matter of Life and Death   25
Ballymena Academy   28

Part 2: Wartime Diaries 1939–1942   **31**
Everything Seems All Up   33
Honor's Diary   37
Birthday Letters   50

Part 3: My Family 1951–1975 55
The Lark in the Clear Air 57
Golden Hair 59
The Quiet American 65
The Windsor Question 70
The Twelfth 74
Angels and Ghosts 79
Words and Music 83
Ballybradden (ii) 87
A Foreign Country 92
Cockles and Mussels 95
Climb Every Mountain 99
Ein Aber Bitte 103
La Gloire de Mon Père 107
'We're Gonna Fix Yer Da' 111
Son of a Preacher Man 113
God Only Knows/I'm a Believer 116
The Big Man 120
Wearing the Right Collar 126
Maintenant on parle français 129

Part 4: My Story 1975–1983 139
Goodbye Yellow Brick Road 141
Ulster Strikes Again 146
L'Été Indien 149
What a Difference a D Makes 155
The Road to Dublin 159
Iona 163
The Third Secretary 166
Solemnly Meeting the Pope 175
The Wearing of the Green 180

The Girl from Armoy 184
Walking with My Father 187

Part 5: Echoes 2018–2023 **191**
Duke Street 193
Closely Related to Chester 196
Among the Savages 198
Covenanters (ii) 201
Partners 205
JRBH 207
British, Irish or Both 211
Dublin Revisited 213
My Pilgrim Journey 217
The Sky Ablaze (ii) 220
The Corncrake's Welcome (ii) 225
My Belfast 230
My Windsor Framework 235
Caithness 240

Acknowledgements 245
Bibliography 247

Prologue

At the foot of the Lisburn Road in South Belfast, where it forms a T-junction with Sandy Row, is the spot where in 1690 King William of Orange tied his horse on his way to meet King James II at the Boyne. Nearby stands a red-bricked Victorian building, which used to house the Samaritan Hospital. This was where, a little before midnight on Saturday 31 March 1955, when Sir Winston Churchill was the British Prime Minister, and post-war rationing was still in place, my mother went into labour with her second child, me.

Honor Hanna, née Boyd, asked the midwife to alert her husband, Bill, by telephone, not to summon him for the event of my birth, for such was not the practice in those days, but so that he should at least be aware of her forthcoming ordeal and my imminent arrival.

To her dismay, the midwife could not get through to

Windsor Manse, two miles up the road, for my father had taken the phone off the hook, lest he be disturbed from a sound night's sleep before preaching at the Sunday morning service at Windsor Presbyterian Church.

My mother was herself a midwife. She had delivered hundreds of babies in the tenements of Edinburgh's High Street, usually onto pages from the *News of the World*. So she simply got on with her heroic work in the Samaritan, with the assistance of the midwife and a physician. Five hours later, examining the jaundiced fruit of her labour, she agreed with the doctor's observation that I was 'as yellow as a duck's bill', but decided to love me all the same.

Later that Sabbath day, having completed his pastoral duties, my father dandered down the road to see us. My parents decided to call me William, gifting me the Christian name my father had inherited from his father and his father before him. Thus began my lifetime quest to impress my folks and live up to the family name.

Dad was born in 1916 and Mum in 1921, defining years in the history of Ireland. Dad first saw the light of day in Ballybradden, near Loughgiel in County Antrim, in March 1916, a few days before the Easter Uprising in Dublin, and a few months before the Battle of the Somme, at which many Ulstermen, including one of his uncles, were killed. Mum was born in Ahmedabad, India, in August 1921, at the end of the monsoon season. This was the year of the partition of Ireland, and the creation of the new place called Northern Ireland, to which her missionary family returned two years later.

Let's leave me in my cot at hospital, sleeping off my entry into the world, recovering from the first of many

All Fools' Days, while my parents take centre stage. A clergyman and a nurse/midwife – I could scarcely have chosen a more caring couple to be born to. By nature, and by profession, they were bound to look after my spiritual and physical nourishment. Who were they? What were they like? Where did they belong in their divided country?

Fortunately, I have some written material to work with, so that my parents can explain things in their own words. First Dad will describe what it was like to grow up, the eldest of six children, on a small Co. Antrim farm, in a mixed community, in troubled times. He wrote some pages, with my encouragement, in 1981, when he had just retired and was looking back on his life, as one tends to do at that stage. Mum didn't write memoirs, but during her 21st year she kept a diary. I found it in a blue case after she died, and although I don't have her permission to print it, she didn't tell me not to. In Part II I've included extracts from the diary, written in 1942, a fateful year for her family.

It is perhaps unfair of me to place together the considered thoughts of an elderly gentleman, aware of how he wishes posterity to remember him, and the unguarded private diary of the young woman who became his wife. But that's what my parents left me, and since their influence on my life and thinking is second to none, their writing is as good a place as any to start my story.

Each of us lives out our life in places and times that may appear to be interesting or dull, permanent or changing, improving or declining. I happen to have grown up – physically, spiritually, and politically – in an industrial city at the top right-hand corner of a small island on the periphery of Europe, at a time when the place was about to explode. These circumstances forced me to question everything around me – the political, social and religious order. I believe that I am the richer for the experience, even though it wasn't always fun.

The wee place I still call home, Northern Ireland or the North of Ireland, depending on how you look at it, has produced many writers of poetry and prose finer than mine, but that doesn't prevent the rest of us from feeling compelled to tell our own stories. It just encourages us. So here's my tale to add to the pile.

Once my parents have introduced themselves, I'll be back, to take up my own story of growing up in Belfast in the 1960s, coming of age during the Troubles, discovering a wider world outside Northern Ireland, and eventually becoming an Irish and European diplomat.

My parents told me that the first word I uttered was 'cheerio'. So 'cheerio' for now. See you later. WH Junior.

WH
Brussels, 2023

PART ONE

My Father's Story

1921–1936

The Sky Ablaze

It was the Hallowe'en weekend of 1961, and we had taken a family break at the little County Down resort of Ardglass. On the Saturday evening, as darkness fell, I took two small boys for a stroll along a country road. We had no torch, and the only light on our path was provided by the occasional passing car. But happily, it was a night of stars. Millions of stars, it seemed, were sparkling from the edge of the sea right over our heads to the remotest horizons. The two lads simply stood and stared upwards at the heavens. Above them and all around them was a vast panorama of twinkling splendour. The breathless amazement of those two city youngsters sent me back to a time when I was their age, but from a very different background.

***

The small village of Loughgiel lies on the sheltered landward side of the County Antrim hills. The dozens of homesteads clustered along the brae-face look down on larger holdings stretching across a few miles west to Lissanoure Castle, home of the McCartneys, a family once enjoying power and prestige not only in Ireland but much further afield. The first British Ambassador to China was a Lord McCartney, the present family now living in faded echoes of former style. Ten miles to the north is the seaside resort of Ballycastle, and at the same distance west, the market town of Ballymoney. Our home stood mid-way between the brae-side dwellings and the estate. The plantation of County Antrim stopped thereabouts and could be traced in the religious division of the community. A few Church of Ireland families worshipped in the handsome well-built Anglican Church on the edge of the estate. Here on Sundays the voice of Captain George McCartney could be heard reading the lessons. There were a few reformed Presbyterian, Covenanting families like our own, but for the most part this was Roman Catholic country, a religious belt continuing north to Ballycastle.

The year was 1921 and things were not quite normal, nor, for a small boy of five years, were they easy to understand. Our elders largely kept current affairs to themselves, but it was clear even to the very young that the whole country was in a state of turmoil. We could hear talk of strange creatures called 'Black and Tans'. Every lorry filled with men and racing along the road was closely scrutinised, for some carried Union Jacks and some didn't, and we gathered the difference was a vital one. Our home stood at the end of a long lane, which helped to protect us from the full impact.

But then, early one morning, the residence of the local Roman Catholic school teacher was seen to be in flames. We felt at once involved. That gentleman with his wife and family were held in high esteem in the district, and although we learned to our relief that they had all been moved to a safer place, it did mean that something was seriously the matter. Across the fields we ran that day to get a closer look at the blazing house. No fire brigade had been summoned, nor did we then know of the existence of such a thing. As darkness fell on that winter day we went off once again to get a final look through the hedge and over the road. There before our very eyes was the wreckage of a fine house and we could hear the sizzle of the smoking embers as the blackened timbers collapsed. It took us a long time to get to sleep that night.

This episode was an ugly business. It was like a bad dream. And soon it came again, ten days later, early on the Sabbath. After he had been out checking on some animals there was a whispered aside from father to mother, 'It's the Police Barracks this time'. A little later, on our way to church, we saw the devastation of the second building.

Things were puzzling. We heard the odd-sounding word 'curfew' being used regularly. And there were stories of strange men calling at farm-houses and taking possession of shot-guns, with a stern warning not to report the loss for a number of hours. This happened in our home when Mother was alone minding some sleeping children upstairs. She did not observe the warning and reported at once to the men milking in the byre, by which time darkness had enveloped the retreating visitors. Some people calling at our house talked about dark ominous deeds in places like Derry and Dublin. One phrase that lingered in my memory was 'Dublin and the half of Derry'. I chewed over that phrase, but no light would come on the meaning.

Gradually it dawned upon us that the commotion in the country had some sort of religious connotation. That was hard to take in. For we had good and friendly Roman Catholic neighbours, many of whom were in the habit of calling regularly at our home. Was it not in a Roman Catholic house over at Glenbush that I had seen and tasted my first tomato? And did not the Parish Priest Father Healey greet our family most warmly every time we met him on the road?

On both sides we continued to meet and act normally. Moreover the Troubles were discussed with our visitors. On one occasion when the matter of the guns was brought up it was quickly pointed out that none of the men of Loughgiel were involved. The deed had been done by 'fellows over the hill'.

One Catholic family had always been special visitors. Seven sons and daughters presided over by a venerable matron, a widow since the birth of her youngest. They visited us and we them several times each week. One son entered the priesthood, from a parish that produced five such candidates in my earlier years. When this genial young man came home on holiday he loved to make a parade of the Latin he had acquired at college. Young Father Daniel was also in some demand as a referee at any local hurling match that might befall. From time to time we saw him in action on the Sabbath afternoon, though we were not supposed to be watching any form of recreation on that day. But the sight was well worth seeing. Clad in his full cassock *he paraded along the touchline blowing a vociferous whistle. Only occasionally, when some ruling was questioned by the players, did he slide imperiously on to the playing pitch. And that was that. His mother was a remarkable lady, deeply devout. She never allowed us children to leave her home after a visit without imparting a benediction on small, puzzled Protestant heads. She it was, years afterwards, who, with her own hands and her deft crochet needles, produced in time for my ordination my first and only silk cassock, a work of art and beauty. On receiving my profuse thanks her only reply was, 'All I ask is that you remember me in your prayers'.*

Winter always seemed to bring us frost and snow, which provided not only snowmen and snowballing but also a horse-drawn sleigh-ride through the undulating lanes and slopes of the fields. There was the cosy security of the farm kitchen in the long dark evenings, with oil-lamps and turf-fires and the jolly 'craic' as neighbours and visitors dropped in for a while — the younger children being packed off early to bed, while the older ones were permitted to listen for an hour longer. In the farm buildings outside there was the occasional distant stamp from a horse in the stable; the delirious excitement when a foal was born in the loose-box specially prepared for the event, or the birth of a calf in the byre. The lambs came later, sometimes as late as St Patrick's Day, but their advent was greeted with the same emotion. The new lambs were steadily counted, until the knowledgeable among us could announce, 'One more single and maybe a pair of twins, and that's all for this year'.

If winter held these compensations, it was for summer we really lived. Summer brought the long school holidays and the long evenings, and hopefully the long carefree days. One never felt like climbing a tree in winter, but as soon as the foliage was full blown we clambered up among the leafy branches and built our own wee homes to which only the specially invited were welcome. Dream homes they were. We never used the words 'Let's pretend'. The whole business was quite serious, as far as we were concerned.

Around our farm-house there was a shelter belt of ash, sycamore and chestnut trees near the tall tops of which the crows annually nested. The fact that the nests were slung so high was sufficient incentive. We knew how to make a sling and there was plenty of ammunition. Mercifully casualties were few. But we had the satisfaction of causing much alarm among those broody crows.

Still less reputable was our venture into the mysteries of nicotine. Woodbine was the cigarette commonly in use in our district and the price of a packet was scarcely prohibitive. Secrecy from prying eyes was crucial. The secluded spot in a nearby stack-yard was our chosen venue. However, 'the best laid schemes gang aft a-gley'. Our summer evening brought us a near disaster. A carelessly flung match landed on a hay-rick, and to our shock and horror in a few seconds we had flames and destruction of precious hay. Had it been one of the large stacks nearby, the mind boggles. As it turned out, our frenzied efforts to extinguish the blaze quickly brought us assistance. At this point the veil of memory kindly descends. But we do recall that our merited punishment was verbal rather than corporal. Some parents take the longer view.

We had a two-mile meander home from school each afternoon. Often we made the journey in the company of others from the neighbouring Roman Catholic school.

We were good friends and often used to compare notes on educational matters. One afternoon during the season when the benweed was in full bloom we pulled a few hefty specimens from the side of the road and staged a mock battle. It was great fun. The next afternoon at the same time and place we continued where we had left off, this time with a deal more skill and venom. Veterans in the art of benweed warfare we had now become, and our third engagement was as near the real thing as may be. As we repaired home to bathe or conceal our battle scars it was clear to both sides that some kind of crisis was looming. We learned that on the following day the mother of one of our friendly protagonists intended to conceal herself behind a hedge at a strategic point and await further developments. As it happened, we already knew a fair bit about the reputation of this lady. The end came quickly. Hostilities ceased forthwith. And the armistice held.

Covenanters

We were Reformed Presbyterians. What that signified would engage our minds only in later years. To us children the outward evidences were the singing of the Metrical Psalms to the total exclusion of all other spiritual songs, the singing being led by a choir of three men who stood while the congregation remained seated; lengthy prayers taken by the minister but while the congregation remained seated and turning their backs on the pulpit (a relic of the grim 'persecuting times' in the Scottish highlands and glens); a full diet of worship which included a sermon, heavy and deeply concerned with our distinctive interpretation of the Bible; and a very strict observance of the Lord's Day.

The Reformed Presbyterian Church tended to discourage its members from political activity and from membership of Secret Societies. Also from enlistment in the forces of the Crown. My maternal Grandfather was an elder of the church, *but from his family, two sons had joined up in the Kaiser's war. This fact, we were later given to understand, caused some estrangement and a breach in church fellowship. The old man declared that he would never leave the Reformed Presbyterian Church and encouraged his family to continue to attend the 'Meeting House' but as for himself, he would worship God on the Sabbath by reading his Bible and saying his own prayers at home.*

I hold two contrasting memories of that Grand-Sire. I remember the day when he drove the five miles to our home in pony and trap to inspect some cattle that he understood were for sale. He made a quick inspection and enquired the price. My father replied that the animals were not quite ready for sale and that he intended to retain them for a few more weeks. Turning on his heel the old man went back to the farmyard, yoked up the pony and trap, and drove straight home. He felt strongly that his journey had been undertaken under false pretences. We had seen evidence of his quick and determined spirit.

The other memory is more poignant. On his death bed, at his request, two of us senior grandchildren were ushered into his room. He first asked for the 23rd Psalm to be read, which reading he accompanied with fading voice. Then, clad in his night-gown and wearing a skull comfort cap, he called us over to his bedside. Laying a feeble hand on each of our heads he imparted a favourite Old Testament Benediction, which remains with us to enshrine his memory.

Soon after the old man's death the family broke away from the Reformed Church and joined the Presbyterian Church in Ireland.

It was almost a traumatic experience for children. We

*had to adapt to a new style of service on the Sabbath. Now
we remained seated during the prayers and the singing was
led by a mixed choir of about a dozen voices. No organ
had so far been introduced and the keynote for the singing
was provided by a Precentor, complete with pitch pipe, a
wondrous little gadget for which we came to have a great
respect. The shrill voices of the sopranos at once took up the
melody of the tune and the others closed in on them. We
were glad of those other accompanying voices, accustomed
as we were to men only. The deeper voices of the altos and
then male bass gave a sense of balance. And rounding off the
whole effort we had the tenors led by the Precentor himself,
a Scot from Dumfriesshire who was the game keeper at the
Lissanoure estate.*

*Hymns were gradually making an appearance in this
congregation but were saved for special occasions. However,
we had the singing of scriptural paraphrases and a wide array
of new tunes in which members of the congregation joined
heartily. Just across the aisle from our allotted pew was a
retired School Principal whose magnificent bass thrilled us
as he gave full voice to his part in 'Duke Street', 'Glasgow'
and 'Wiltshire'. He did not need to look down at his Tonic
Solfah music. He knew them all.*

*We travelled to Ballyweaney Church via the Corkey
Road past our first school, and always we returned by the
Loughgiel Road alongside part of the Lissanoure Estate. That
homeward jaunt became a weekly delight. Most members
journeyed to and fro by pony and trap. Others residing near
to the church walked. It meant that the pedestrians on our
road had already dandered slowly up the first gentle slopes
and were dispersing to their various homes before the horse-*

drawn vehicles were on their way. But we had our reward. Walking with the others and wheeling his bike, which was adorned with every type of gadget including gears, was the Precentor himself. As we drew alongside, he mounted his bicycle, and pulling in on our right, he placed one hand on the bumper board of the trap, greeted us, and then proceeded to his weekly conversation with our parents. We were privileged indeed. That rich inimitable lowland Scots accent held us spellbound. Oh, those stories from his native land. We had Harry Lauder all to ourselves. Nobody wanted to rush that Sabbath journey home. Too soon, alas, it was over as we reached the entrance of the Estate; with a gentlemanly doffing of his hat to the lady present our genial friend was on his way to his own home and Sunday dinner.

The Corncrake's Welcome

Only five miles from our home, on the 9th of June each year, at the village of Cloughmills, there took place the first fair of the year. We never missed it. It was there, amid the sheep and the cattle and the stalls, with little groups of men around each Public House, that I saw my first adult fist fight, an ugly business and bloody. Two inebriated farmers had got on the wrong side of each other, and the matter was settled there and then on the side of the road, with plenty of onlookers. Why did someone not intervene and stop it? I was distressed and puzzled. Fortunately it was an isolated incident in an otherwise happy day.

The journey home from the fair was by pony and trap and was always a leisurely business. And indeed, why hurry? There was so much to talk about after an exciting day out. Often it was the twilight hour before the home avenue was reached. Then as the weary pony slowed down to walk the last stretch of lane, sometimes it happened. Halt and listen! While the rising moon shed her benison over the quiet countryside lying in the shadows, and the twinkling lights of dwellings in the braeside flickered fitfully, the stilly night was suddenly shattered. A couple of corncrakes in full voice! Were they hoarsely protesting that we had disturbed them? Or were they giving us a welcome home? No matter, it was lovely to listen to. The poet Keats may have celebrated the soprano of the nightingale; we preferred the throaty basso of the Crex Crex. The crake was our song-bird. We were home again.

Standing exactly a mile as the crow flies from our home, Lissanoure Castle held mystery for us. The place drew us children, as by a magnet. There was extensive forestation in addition to hills, valleys and several lakes. The big house on the hill had been the ancestral home of the McCartneys for several generations. Unfortunately, in 1847, a barrel of gunpowder accidentally exploded, resulting in the death of a member of the family and serious structural damage. It must have been quite a blast for the reverberation was felt over a wide area, including by an ancestor of ours who was at that moment atop a corn stack.

Thereafter the McCartneys built a lodge, pleasantly situated on the shore of the main lake. The shrub-covered islands on the lake, we noticed, were most convenient for the concealment of shooting butts, and the regular shoots at the lodge were of keen interest to lesser sportsmen who operated beyond the fringes of the estate. The early morning crescendo of firing sent scores of wild duck and game fleeing to safety in the surrounding countryside. Once there, unfortunately, they had to run the gauntlet of other local marksmen.

I can so clearly recall one evening as we travelled on the country road adjoining the lake meeting a shooting party from the lodge, led by Captain McCartney himself. Each man carried a gun and the gun carried by the captain was white-barrelled, or at least it seemed so to me. I wouldn't deny that the evening sun glinting through the trees may have been shining on the gun.

Just outside the estate, in the centre of a fine arable ten-acre field, stood the imposing knoll, visible for many miles, of Gallows Hill. How many of these do we have in Ulster?

A visitor travelling round the lake of Lissanoure, along the tree-lined road and up the gentle slope to Lavin Hill, may stop at the top and pause to admire the view. Westwards lies Ballymoney, beyond that Coleraine, and in the dim far distance the outline of the Sperrins. But first at the foot of the hill lies the Route country, centered on the parish of Kilraughts. Here lived many friends and relatives. Here stood the Presbyterian Church and the Reformed Presbyterian Church and the school called Knockahollet, and all the townlands bore names that would signify more and more to us — Craigtempon, Drumabest, Knockanavery, Ganaby, Topp, Cubbunhall, Ballynagashel, Tober and Pharis.

Our father had the good sense to marry a lady from Kilraughts. From a covenanting family of nine sons and daughters, she brought to our home and district a wider outlook and a new dimension. Practical to her fingertips, she was also a dreamer of dreams, largely centred on her family. She was schooled at Ballymoney Intermediate by a team of first-rate teachers and her prize copy of the works of William Shakespeare is still in our treasured possession. Her command of Latin and mathematics became an ever-present help when our turn came to tackle those horrors. Her writing hand was a joy to read till the very end of her life. As a family we blessed the day that father went 'over the hill' to bring mother to our home.

With much less educational benefit, our father set an example of industry that remains with us. If he had a fault it was that of being a workaholic. With a minimum of help he toiled at the task of mixed farming, early and late. In his rare off-moments we all enjoyed his flair as a raconteur. Home from a shopping expedition in Cloughmills or Ballymoney, he would first change into his working clothes and then for fifteen minutes or so he would regale us with the latest news from the market town. That was something special. But he could also listen, if need be. One late evening visitor finally took his leave of us. As a token of gratitude, the head of the house put on his hat to convey the caller to the end of the lane, a distance of some 300 yards. It turned out to be a lengthy business and as some of us retired to bed we overheard the explanation: 'I had to stand at the end of that lane till Johnny sold the ten sheep all over again'. At the funeral service for my father the clergyman said, 'This man was a great encourager'.

There were six children in our family, four boys and two girls. Of these only four were to survive into adulthood. The deaths of a beloved sister at 16 years of age and an adorable youngest brother at five years created an aching void in our lives which was so painful as to be almost tangible, though as children we never discussed the matter. Here was a salutary reminder that life is a precious gift, not to be taken for granted. Doubtless too, over the years, it bound those of us who remained more closely together.

Ballybradden

For several generations our family had lived on a farm of some 55 acres of arable land and a further 15 acres which included a productive turf bog. There was thus a yearly cycle of farming activity for all able-bodied sons of six years and upwards — no heavy compulsion, but there was the expectation that all would lend a hand. Nor was it all a burden and a chore, for who would so describe work in a hay field, culminating in the delight of a ride on the hay cart? As the cart rumbled its way along rough lanes, even the horse between the shafts seemed to enter into the spirit of the thing. The same applied to the tying of the sheaves of corn when the crop was ready for harvesting. But not quite so pleasurable for us was the gathering of potatoes, for that was usually in October or later, and the light relief of a potato gathering holiday from school did not compensate for the cold on the fingers and the back pains from continual stooping and lifting.

The turf bog was another ball game. For this time-honoured occupation good weather was essential. The walk across the fields to the turf bank on all manner of errands, ranging from teatime baskets to bandages for injured hands, or messages received during the day at the farmhouse, was most congenial to youthful assistants. The actual job of cutting on the turf bank was for older and stronger hands. Only a grown man could skillfully wield the curiously shaped peat spade, or deftly arrange the sods of peat on the slipe, to be horse-drawn to the place selected for spreading and drying. The later work could be negotiated by younger people as the turf advanced into the ruckle and clamp stages. Best of all was the carting home of the finished product. It meant that we had winter fuel for another year.

How times have changed for us all in the last fifty years, and how different, even to the casual eye, the appearance of a typical Ulster farm. Manual labour has been reduced to a minimum. Clydesdale horses have given way to the tractor, the combine harvester and a whole variety of complicated machinery. Strip grazing has replaced the old-fashioned fencing of fields. Chemical fertilizers have encroached heavily on the former organic method. Flocks and herds are larger and better organized. Barley has taken over from oats. In general farms have a more business-like appearance. But one casualty of the times has been the once lucrative flax crop, providing the fibre for the linen industry for which Ulster was famed the world over. That most colourful of all farming sights, the gentle billowing in the breeze of the bluebell and the whitebell over carefully cultured acres is, alas, no more. Possibly only in some hidden corners of Belgium or France could we find it today. Let's hope the day of the flax will *return. Although not the easiest of crops to handle, flax held a fascination for every mixed farmer, and something for his bank balance as well.*

There was no escape from the chore of pulling and separating the flax boughs manually. How often in our home had we been told of the efforts of a local farmer, who was a bit of an eccentric and a genius, to invent a mechanical answer to this tangled problem. It was alleged that his machine could pull the lint, but, in spite of his best endeavours, the seemingly simple task of separating the boughs baffled him. The poor man took it badly to heart. His end was untimely.

Our local rector had two fine sons, very popular in the community. Another young fellow, a friend of the two, joined them on a summer holiday at the Rectory. One hot day the three lads went off for a bathe in a nearby river. As he plunged into the cold fresh water the visitor caught a nasty cramp, and, despite repeated and desperate efforts by the two brothers, he drowned. Naturally the two boys were deeply distraught. Tragedy had struck in the summer sun, and over the next few weeks their parents became really concerned about them. Then their mother, in a conversation with my father, came up with an idea to lift the minds of the two young men from the recent calamity. We had a five-acre field of flax ready for the pulling. What did these two know about flax pulling? Hardly a thing. They had no experience whatever. 'Send them over to me tomorrow morning. I'll look after them,' said my father. And they duly reported for work. The other workers in the field were fully aware of the circumstances, and they took a liberal view of the inexpert manoeuvres of the young fellows of the Rectory. Manfully the boys stuck to their uncongenial task, until at last the crop was ready for transporting to the retting dam, there to be carefully submerged with stones, the next essential state in the harvesting of the fibre. At this point their labours ceased. They were excused from the smelly business a week later, of rescuing the sodden 'beets' of lint from their cold bath, prior to spreading thinly on the adjacent field, to receive the maturing benefit of sun and breeze. Many were the expressions of gratitude from the Rector and his wife, so long as they remained in the parish of Loughgiel, for the imaginative answer to their cry for help.

Wireless

***

It was a Saturday in late winter in the early 1930s. A kinsman had taken the day off to supervise the operation. First he erected a pole on the roof high alongside our dwelling. He bored a hole through the timber of a window, produced a wire to be attached to the pole, threaded it through the window, and finally secured it to a strange looking contraption with lots of knobs and dials. And we now owned our first wireless. This was no crystal set but the real thing. It was mid-afternoon and the voice of the rugby commentator from Cardiff was saying, 'Ross has crossed the Welsh line for his second score. The conversion is now being attempted. Square two.' A reference to the diagram of the field was then provided for listeners. The player was William Ross. His performance that day has been equalled by few Irishmen.

At school some companions talked about 'the flicks'.

But we lived miles away from the nearest picture house. We didn't have the money or transport, nor would there have been much encouragement from our parents for such waste of time on a Friday evening or a Saturday afternoon matinee. After all, the outside world came right to our own fireside through the wireless.

At first, we listened to music broadcast from England: Jack Payne and his band, Henry Hall and his Orchestra, and Reginald Dixon at the organ of the Blackpool Tower Ballroom.

Religion too had a place on the air. One young Scottish preacher from Govan Old Parish Church, George MacLeod, was compelling. This man could talk and what he had to say was important. There was a Thursday evening short service from St Michael's, Chester Square in London. And also from St Martin in the Fields. We loved the Irish witticisms of Reverend Pat McCormack and later the passionate pleading of his successor, Reverend Dick Sheppard.

Jamie McAleese was the local carpenter and very competent. Our family would call him in to build an extension to the kitchen or to erect a new barn. His wife was a teacher, and their home was a delight to visit. It was so neat and tidy and ordered. To boys accustomed to the daily disarray of a busy farmhouse, this home looked different. Different too was the choice of wireless programmes that always caught the ear on entering. Tuned in twice daily to London, we were used to solid and substantial fare, whereas the McAleese apparatus always seemed to carry the sounds of a Ceilidh. We soon learned to tune in to Radio Athlone. There was always gaiety about the daily output on the Southern waves. When John McCormack was not singing the evocative melodies of Thomas Moore, a Ceilidh band set our feet tapping. To add to the novelty there was a generous quota of programmes in the Gaelic tongue.

Around eleven o'clock each evening, the lady announcer from Athlone signed off in English and in Gaelic with 'and that, ladies and gentlemen, is the end of broadcasting for today'. I heard this so often I learnt it by heart: 'agus sin deireadh'. I have often spoken this one phrase in Irish, and it has served me well as a useful variant for the more traditional 'goodbye'.

A Matter of Life
and Death

Country children live close to nature, and by that token, are continually in the presence of the great twin mysteries — Life and Death. Each springtime throbs with the thrill of new birth in flock or herd, in sty or stable, and almost as often we are confronted by the enemy of life, that dark hovering angel whose command is halt. Most parents take steps to shield their offspring from the morbid. But what can they do when from neighbouring fields men down tools and rush to help rescue a bullock drowning in a swamp, and all their united efforts are too late to save the animal? And when a favourite working horse comes to the end of its days and expires, the whole household assumes the aspect of mourning, as for a dear friend. We knew such things at first hand, all too often.

We had also been distant spectators of many funerals, proceeding to the graveyard adjoining the local Roman Catholic chapel. Even from several hundred yards away, we found a spectacular dignity about these occasions: the solemn tolling of the bell as the cortege neared its destination, the procession of pedestrians, the walking cyclists, the long line of ponies and traps, and, towering higher than the rest, the splendid gleaming black hearse. All eyes were on the two coachmen, seated high in front. We noticed that the prominent white shoulder scarf worn by one of the two on the way to the burial ground was later removed on the homeward journey. All this we witnessed again and again as spectators.

The day came when we were more intimately involved. A roadside accident had proved fatal and plunged some friends of our family into deep grief. The young man concerned was a student for the Ministry of the Reformed Presbyterian Church. He had just completed a session in Belfast and was on his way back home. Leaving the train at Ballymoney, he picked up a bicycle to complete the remaining six miles of his journey. Almost within sight of home and a big welcome from his proud family, a passing car struck.

Next evening, we went along to the home. Our parents thought that the two eldest children were old enough to accompany them. It was our first experience of a house in mourning — strange and at first unnerving. These people were cousins on our father's side. Their farmhouse was a dream, beautifully maintained and always filled with the laughter of bright lovely people. The sisters and brother loved to entertain and never had we known a dull moment on any previous visit. This time was different. A solemn hush pervaded every room. *Even the family dog and cat seemed subdued. Voices were lowered to a whisper and tears flowed freely. But there were no hysterics and no loud emotional display. After the first few minutes, while our parents expressed their sympathy with the bereaved family, we younger ones were ushered to another room. But we were not left on our own. The younger sister of the family joined us. We could see from her eyes the evidence of many tears. But not a word of her grief did she mention. She simply chatted. She talked with us about anything and everything that she thought might interest us, apart from the one subject that we knew was being discussed next door. I have a faint recollection that she even produced a game of Snakes and Ladders. Her thoughtfulness was more than somewhat. That far distant sad evening remains, etched in dark silk dresses and black suits and quiet voices: the backdrop to a deep sorrow, borne with touching dignity.*

Ballymena Academy

At Knockahollet school, a friend and I had often light-heartedly talked about our futures. Farmers' sons both, neither of us felt strongly drawn towards the agricultural process. But we were unanimous about the best alternative. We both wanted to get into banking. That neither of us became bankers is irrelevant. We had at least found an incentive to proceed to second level education. We were fortunate to have the backing of our parents. By their unselfish support over the next ten years, they were making a huge sacrifice. Often, I wonder if we fully expressed our gratitude.

Vividly, I recall September 1929. The weather was fine and harvesting operations were in full swing all over County Antrim. Half the population of Ballymena Academy were farmers' sons, but they would have little or no part in bringing in the sheaves. Scores of new boys from the country *had entered the school for the first time and already the truth was dawning for them. The unwritten motto of the school was 'Workers only admitted'. That thrifty Scottish area round the Braid would only support an institution that gave results. And the brothers Fullerton had produced a school which did just that.*

We had been in attendance for just two weeks, and the afternoon clock was pointing to half past two. Only one further period of the school day remained. In 40 minutes, bells would ring, doors would open, and youthful prisoners would escape in all directions. The mixed class of 28 inmates of B2 room could hardly wait for it. In the course of a single fortnight, we had been confronted with our future — a vast uncharted land of algebra, trigonometry, French and Latin, with a dash of science thrown in for good measure. And to compound it all, homework was compulsory in all classes. All members of staff insisted on this evidence of proper assimilation. For the foreseeable future we were going to shoulder the burden of four to five hours' preparation. My afternoon reverie was shattered by the sound of a precise voice at my elbow.

'Hanna, haven't seen you yet at rugby practice. Get hold of some togs for tomorrow afternoon.' The speaker was the games master who was also my form master. There was no escape. The togs were duly procured and donned.

Fifty years later I bless the day when that quiet peremptory command was uttered in my ear. True, I have never worn the Red Hand of Ulster or the Green Jersey of Ireland, but the game has proved of immense enrichment. Although as a spectacle rugby looks rough and tough, it embodies some of the most valuable qualities in the field of sport; it puts a minimum on individualism and a premium on brotherhood. My own debt to the game is life-long. I number my rugby friends in hundreds.

PART TWO

Wartime Diaries

1939-1942

Everything Seems All Up

Dad's memoirs stop at the point where he goes to university. He does not explain what led him to abandon the idea of banking and decide instead to train for the ministry. He was no doubt influenced by his Uncle Sam Hanna, his father's brother, who became a medical doctor and later the minister of Berry Street Presbyterian Congregation in Belfast. Uncle Sam often visited the farm at Ballybradden and took a keen interest in his nephew's upbringing.

Nor did Dad record much about his religious calling. There doesn't seem to have been a sudden moment of illumination, just a growing realisation that he was called to be a minister. It was a vocation his parents encouraged. A colleague, John Barclay, recalled many years later the words Dad used at his ordination as a minister in 1939.

'Today I remember the rock from which I am hewn.

For I cannot but reflect how little I owe to myself for my present position. And if I owe little to myself, my debt to those with whom I have to do is accordingly increased. If there is, humanly speaking, any credit due on my side to the fact that I am standing here today, give that credit not to me, but rather to my father and mother... for the Christian home they created, for their quiet example of steadfast faith in God, through the years of toil and the sweat known only to themselves and Him who shall one day reward them.'

Dad spent three years at Magee College in Derry, where he showed promise in the debating society and on the rugby field, and a year at New College, Edinburgh University, where he shared digs with another young Ulsterman destined for the ministry, Ray Davey. Dad and Ray played rugby for the University 1st XV, who were Scottish University Champions in 1936/7. Ray was my mother's cousin, but I don't think Mum and Dad met until well after the war.

Dad's first position was as Assistant Minister of Mountpottinger Presbyterian Church in a working-class area of East Belfast. His diary records his banal clerical work, as Europe was once more on the brink of war.

Thursday 31 August 1939

A lazy kind of day. My cold somewhat better. Good sleep last night. Trying to settle to write a prayer. But settle I cannot. Invited Mr and Mrs M to tea. Conversation a bit slow at start but warmed considerably when we found each other's depth. Parted in good form.

Friday 1 September

What about a week's typing of all the name cards or even ten days? A nice little children's address? Do I send the Sabbath notice to the Telegraph again?

Very serious international situation this morning. Fighting between Germany and Poland. Hardly know where we stand. Everything seems all up. Only a miracle can prevent a catastrophe. Blackout in Belfast.

Saturday 2 September

Morning papers tell of heavy German Polish fighting. Had dinner then went out in the car for a run. Donaghadee, Bangor, then Helen's Bay. Had to prepare Sunday school lesson. And so to bed.

Sunday 3 September

Morning service. Not taking any part today, except Sunday school in afternoon. Very glad, as remains of cold still here. Britain declared war at 11 a.m. Very tense atmosphere in church. Moses Alexander very good and helpful. Fierce electric storm this afternoon. Evening service good attendance.

Dad's writing was never easy to read, and there is more in this diary than I can decipher. He himself had difficulty reading his handwritten sermons, and used to commit them to heart, using the written text as a prop. In 1940 he was called to be minister in the Co Antrim town of Randalstown, where he lived, looked after his parishioners and played rugby for the next nine years. As I have no written record of that time we will turn to my mother's story. Although it was written eighty years ago, it has an immediacy that time cannot erase.

Honor's Diary

Many of the letters that I published in *Voyages with My Grandfather* were written by Grandfather Boyd to his fifteen-year-old daughter Honor, who was destined to become my mother. He called her Eyebright, after a wildflower, and urged her to 'keep plugging away' at her lessons. She was not academically inclined and, as the war began, she chose to serve as a student nurse at the Royal Victoria Hospital in Belfast.

In 1941 German bombers blitzed Belfast, destroying vast swathes of the city. Over a thousand people were killed and many more were injured. In her recent novel, *These Days*, Lucy Caldwell writes about young women from a middle-class Belfast family caught up in the destruction and confusion of the Blitz. I would have liked to show the book to Mum and ask her about that time. I asked Uncle Billy what he remembered. He recalled the wail of the sirens and the *ack ack* of the anti-aircraft battery stationed at Balmoral, near their home in Osborne Park. He reminded me that during the air raids the family hid under the dinner table where I am writing now. Uncle Billy envied his elder brother Robin, who was able to leave the house when the raids began and join civil defence personnel.

In 1942 Mum decided to keep a diary. Perhaps she thought the year of her 21st birthday would be special and should be recorded. She wrote in a more legible hand than my father, and I've been able to decipher most of her tale of the life of a young nurse in wartime Belfast. It was heavy work, with long hours and poor pay. Her thoughts often turned to her elder brother Jack, born, like her, in India, and who had returned there as an officer in the Indian Army. His regiment had been sent to Burma to defend the British Empire against the Japanese attack. They were poorly equipped, and their situation was desperate.

Thursday 1 January

The New Year started early and busily. Wilfred called in at 2 a.m. He and Ann had been seeing the New Year in. Not too much in the way of drinks. Finished my slip and am very thrilled with it. Only three coupons. Rather chic, with a piece of the lace of the same colour to form gathered part at top. Met Ann and Joan at Tea Shop. Coffee on me. Went to Robinson and Cleaver's. Got my month's pay. Oh to be a millionaire.

Saturday 3 January

I was very weary after 29 hours with only two in bed.

So I lay in until Selina got up and we had breakfast in bed. The next thing I knew was Edith at the door with her 'May I come in' and found it was dinner time! I got up and as Mummy had gone to see cousins Katy and Lily I made the tea, dusted, etc. and then got at the machine. However, it cleared up and Daddy and I went for a stroll out the Malone Road. Robin and I set off to A. J. Hanna's aunts. Ian was there and Kenneth, a spoilt little thing, but rather winning all the same. We played darts, bagatelle, etc. Tea was pre-war! Thinking of Jack in Burma & so to bed.

Sunday 4 January

Got up at a slightly earlier hour, but after some hymn singing there wasn't much time until we got ready for church. It was very cold and wet and the drawing room fire was welcome and a chicken from Killeen — when will we have such a treat again? Robin brought me back in the car, so I didn't have to leave until 1.45. And so to bed, where I am writing this.

Monday 5 January

A nice night if we hadn't got into a row about not having a man from Observation bed-bathed. Dr K admitted him and then of course at 4 am sent him up to ward 14. Diana near blew me out. Day rather spoilt by worrying about last night's scolding. Got up in fear and trembling but wasn't charged after all. 15 and 16 had a wild take in, German plane over Stormont and 9 bad injuries in and many others. Fairly busy night.

Tuesday 6 January

We had a medicine lecture from 8–9, very interesting but depressing. Extern quite nice but rather slow in getting cleaned up. Wilfred has just been in. He and Ann seem to have had a lovely day in Dublin and done a good deal of shopping. I wish I had someone as crazy about me!

Wednesday 7 January

Next agitation: a fur-trimmed hat belonging to a Mrs Fry has disappeared. Have visions of me having to fork out, hope it will blow over. Went to bed very early as we had to get up to have our photographs taken and parade in front of board to get my prize for hygiene. 1 pound book token, which I feel ought to be spent on my medicine books and yet would like to spend on something more exciting.

Thursday 8 January

Dr K was in and let McCush and me each put a suture into a man's forehead. Quite a thrill! I was up in ward 6 until 6.15. Had a long September letter from Jack. Prayers be with him in Burma.

Friday 9 January

Off to Portballintrae. Hot bath, pack cases and ready for the road at 9.45. Very cold and I slept part of the way. Was sorry for crossness to Mummy, must try harder. House cosy. Very sweet little room overlooking the bay. So warm inside and wintry outside. Ann was off with Wilfred. I think it's a pity they go around so much by themselves. Ann and I walked to church. She asked me to be bridesmaid. I really have had a delightful weekend, thank you God.

Tuesday 3 February

Read over my notes and walked down to Queen's. The exam was fair. Daddy and I went and had a nice tea. New doctors and pupils in extern. Dr G is absolutely stupid in my opinion, and as for the lady pupil... Went for my monthly pay. 1 pound and one shilling, aren't we coming on! We got in a very bad motor accident. The man had two compound fractures on his legs and a head injury. Dr G is so very slow. I should like to stick a pin in him.

Sunday 8 February

We had nice tea and quiet hymn singing evening. Went to Methodist Church and heard the Air Force Chaplain. There was an Air Force choir.

Wednesday 11 February

Joan rang and asked if I would come to a tea dance. The difficulty is they are men short! I'd love to go but don't know if I can manage it. In a terribly bad temper. Congregational meeting. Cold walk there and back in raging bad form. Writing it now I'm ashamed of myself but have been feeling very dull and would like some excitement!

Friday 13 February

Mummy and Daddy went to Armagh. I ironed a few

oddments, sewed the sleeves of my two navy blue coats, and answered the telephone which was a cable from Jack in Rangoon. Safe and well.

Wednesday 18 February
What a night, rush rush rush. 25 women and 27 men most of whom seemed to be mad. I was gazing hopelessly at my urine labels when Dr McK put his arm round me and said: 'Don't worry, Honor, it will all be the same in 100 years'. Somehow it cheered me up.

Thursday 19 February
A lie in bed attempting to revise. Had dreams of cows whose milk must not contain more than 330.000 bacteria. Letter from Jack. He is now an acting captain. I'm so thrilled. If only reinforcements would arrive in Burma.

We had a very hectic night in 7–8. We took in two men, one of whom died.

Friday 20 February
Back to Extern. A hectic take-in into 9 and 10. Three appendices and a bad bus accident. M seems to have spent most of the night in a side ward with Dr S. Really anyone she wants she just has to look at and they fall. Knitted Billy's pullover.

Wednesday 4 March
Ann rang up in a great state. Wilfred has been called up to report on 5th. Special license etc.

Thursday 5 March

M rushed in hysterically and I realised we had both passed. Such a relief. She came in and spent 5–7 with me. I was very annoyed with her remarks about C and said more than I might maybe. She keeps in such top form and talks and talks and talks men. It is getting rather on my nerves. Am now waiting for a bath.

Monday 9 March

Sister off. A rather hectic morning with everyone getting on everyone else's nerves. Surgery lecture. M flapping around. Decided to go to bed very early and sew. I seem to be the safety valve for so many romances. Rangoon has fallen, and I feel very depressed. God keep Jack.

Tuesday 10 March

Had a hectic afternoon with Carson trying to get out of bed all the time, and a man coming out of his anaesthetic, and then Dr S ordered an enema. I could have shot him.

Wilfred thanked me for my present. He asked me to look after Ann should anything happen to him. They are ridiculously happy. We chose our bouquets at Dixons. Ann's tulips pink and mine red.

Tuesday 17 March

Am getting so excited about the wedding. Wilfred and Ann deliriously happy. Wilfred gave me a lovely string of pearls. Lay late in bed though I didn't sleep after 7 with excitement. Frock looks very nice and Wilfred's pearls just make it.

Thursday 19 March

Ann was very calm, cool and collected. Drove to church and she said, 'You know I'm enjoying this'. Rather terrifying walking down the aisle. Very brief service. Mummy says I was too serious walking down the aisle, but it was about Ann, after all. Very nice reception. All the speeches good. Ann looked sweet going away. Wilfred said you always judge a person by their friends and it worked very well both ways with Ann and me.

Saturday 21 March

I went in the car with Mummy and Daddy to Budore. I got willows and Daddy found the first primroses, also there was a lark singing.

Sunday 22 March

Had a 3 o'clock and when I got home Mummy had all prepared for Hilary and Sandy coming to tea.

Hilary came first and then Robin and Sandy who had been out for a walk together. Sandy played beautifully and we all sang some hymns.

Friday 27 March

Senior in male. Were kept fairly busy. Stayed in 2 pm–4 pm break and wrote to Aunt Margaret. Selina came in and we talked some medicine. At night mending. Cold pretty rotten but got to sleep. Please God keep Jack safe.

Saturday 28 March

We were terribly busy. Margaret Mitchell and I took a trolley bus to the end of the lines in our 2–4 break and had a lovely country walk which so invigorated me and helped to clear my cold. We talked congestive heart failure on the way out and just general conversation on the way back. National Day of Prayer. Walked to Great Victoria Street. Rather an odd church built in old-fashioned style but completely modernised with organ like a cinema. What an evening. I had to dig in unaided. Sister did nothing and the three of us were rushed off our feet.

Monday 30 March

Another very hectic day. No extras. 3 ops. Made all the beds and did the laundry before 5 but it was very heavy going. 5–7 surgery lecture, rather interesting, obstructions and appendix. Margaret Mitchell came in at about 9.20 and she and I did quite a lot of medicine. It interests me very much. If only I had more time to do it.

Saturday 4 April

Up in the morning early. Packed, washed, dressed and had breakfast and made my way to the L.M.S station. Robin was home on sick leave and was very useful to me carrying my case etc. It was a crowded train down and was met at station by Daddy, Robin and Billy. House comfortable. In afternoon we walked up behind the Casements. Double summertime began. We were rather late for church which was as usual good. After dinner went to bed feeling rather weary. Evening church and a walk along the miner's road right under Fair Head. Almost like summer.

Monday 6 April
In the morning we walked up one side of Glenshesk and down the other, the rain just kept off all the time. A marvellous afternoon of sunshine. Everything looked spring-like, and the sea was a deep deep blue.

Tuesday 7 April
Another energetic day. We walked to Murlough Bay in the morning. It was a long walk but beautiful. In the evening Mummy and Daddy went to the Cuthberts and we had to entertain the new arrivals, mother and daughter. No inferiority complex there! She just vamps Robin.

Wednesday 8 April
In the morning we walked to Carrick-a-rede. It was fresh and the sun shone most of the way. We all crossed the bridge and explored the island. Robin and Billy had lemonade in the little shop and bought me toffees. After tea we strolled up the old road and Robin and Billy climbed Knocklayde. I wrote to Rosemary and then the vamp enticed us all out for a walk via the Golf Links and back by the shore. I read a little Lorna Doone before bed.

Wednesday 15 April
In the evening went with Mummy to the week of

witness meeting in the Assembly Hall, Christ and the world. Daddy was the main speaker and was as usual simply splendid. Aunt Ena has got safely home from Malaya, but there is no news at all of Uncle Andrew.

Tuesday 21 April

Mummy and I decided to go to Newcastle for the day. We went by train and what a long journey it seemed. It was a glorious day and at Downpatrick the old church was surrounded with a carpet of celandine.

We had our lunch beside the river and both of us said how much Jack would have loved it. After we walked up the Briansford Road I darned two pairs of my black stockings. Then we went down and saw Aunty Wilson. We had tea together and then sat out in the little balcony at the back.

The journey home was quicker, and I decided to risk going home. I'm so glad, for when we arrived, we were met by the shattering news that Jack had been killed in action.

One can hardly believe it and so many little incidents of his life come back to us all. He was a dear brave boy, and now he has given his life for us and others like us.

Uncle Jack and Aunt Charlotte arrived early in the morning. Uncle Willie and Aunt E soon followed. Aunt K even came up from Drogheda. How kind everyone is and all saying the same about Jack, how friendly and loving and kindly he was.

These days just seem like a dream, so many people calling and so many letters arriving. Jack certainly was universally loved. I keep feeling that we are only dreaming this nightmare and that it will pass over. It is terrible to see Daddy's grief. Mummy, I'm sure, will have a reaction later on. I keep thinking of his song, 'but best of all to live your span, it's good to live and be a man'.

Friday 1 May
Staff in the female, fairly light, but very busy at dinner time when sister and I were left to do dinners and make up beds. Sat out in the garden all evening and talked Jack all the time. Daddy had got some lovely photos of him enlarged.

Saturday 2 May
Nice day but poor Mrs Stewart died at 10 p.m. and it was a very heavy job. Had a long letter from Jack. So happy. A captain. General Wavell shaking hands with him.

Tuesday 19 May 1942
My first day in theatre. We did an NBC appendix, a breast. Very interesting and Fleming was such a dear and did practically everything. I just washed instruments and mopped the floor up. P.T didn't notice me at all. Went into town in my 2–4 hoping to see Daddy but he was kept at home by a visitor calling and so I just sat and read and ate Maltesers.

Wednesday 20 May
It was just like old times again and I laddered my

stocking in crossing a barbed wire fence. All up round Nellie's dam. I felt I could talk to Margaret about Jack and she knew and loved him too. I think she will apply for a commission. We had as usual to dash back to be in time for tea, which we weren't. Margaret left me to the bus and we arranged to meet if possible on Friday. She is just the same true friend. Communion in Windsor. It was nice to go again.

Sunday 24 May

Jack's last letter from Burma:

18 March 1942

'*Sitting out here in Burma, where Mars the God of war has his reign. My thoughts keep turning to home and the little things that now mean so much to me, and I find myself wondering if I shall ever see the long blue head of Garron again.*'

Birthday Letters

Rathlin Road
Ballycastle
County Antrim

2/8/42

My dearest Honor,
I have been thinking of you very much all day and wishing
you were here with us. A 21st birthday is such an important
event that it seems all wrong that we can't share it with you.
We are all remembering you and talking about you.

I am sorry that we were so rushed in town on Friday and
that we weren't able to find a satisfactory present. If only Jack
had been here, he would have had a present ready in time for
you. I well remember the day two years ago when he brought
you the purse from Dunbar. On all your birthdays, especially

your 21ˢᵗ, it will remind you of him.

Ballycastle is crowded with memories of him. That awful house 'Homeleigh' brings back so many things that he did and said and especially the first day we saw him in his officer's uniform. In church today I could imagine him joining in the singing. Remember how proud I felt walking with him to church, with his brisk step and his new uniform. Those days do seem very far away, and now there are only four of us to celebrate your birthday 'in absente'.

I wish you every happiness in this year and in all that are to follow. I really do think you are just grand going through with the drudgery of the Royal, while others get easier jobs with more highlights and flag-waving.

Bill and I had a good ride down, 5 hours with several stops for refreshments. Yesterday evening we all went for a walk along the shore. The tennis courts were almost deserted, except for Ernest Clarke who was being coached by his father.

I must stop now as Mother is going out to the post with your letter and I think I will go with her.

Dearest love, and every good wish for many happy years ahead, your loving brother.

Robin

***

My very dear Honor,

All day you have been in my thoughts. We all remembered you this morning and Daddy and I thanked God for giving us our precious daughter. How we have longed to have you here! We shall keep all celebrations until next Sunday. God bless you, dear, with his choicest blessings. The greatest of all is to keep close to Him in happy communion all the time. There is something that no war, or sorrow, or happening of any kind can destroy, and that is God's peace in your heart. It gives one a deep serenity and power that will give help to others. That is what I ask for you today. I do want you to have earthly joy, but above everything I want you to grow more and more in the grace of our Lord Jesus Christ. He adds all other things, and He enriches all earthly joys too.

You have been such a delight to us. It means so much to Dads and the boys to have you. I know Jack is sharing in our thoughts and love of you to-day. More than even loving you for he sees so much more clearly now the highest and best love and is experiencing it.

Many of the relations will be thinking of you too and wishing you every joy and happiness. You will like this house. The view is lovely. Joan and Barbara Hanna are here. We saw them last night and they walked up this length with us. We met many of the old friends here. All were so kind. I feel Jack very near for he loved this place so well. Robin said as he walked last night: 'You see Jack at every corner.' The house is really bright and quite enough room, and you feel the good air gets all round and through it. With a loving hug, darling, and my blessings on you. God be with you always and make you more and more a Blessing.

Your ever-loving Mother.

Did you read the two pages 'For a birthday' at the end of the Daily Light?

This is one of the verses quoted:

'Blessed are they that keep the testimonies and that seek Him with the whole heart.'

***

Dearest Honor,

We are all thinking about you to-day and wishing you were here along with us. It is a wet afternoon and there is a murky haze over everything. Yesterday was a lovely bright day and that helped to make the journey pleasant. We had sunshine and a grand view from here. It is just the opposite of the house we occupied on this road two years ago. The house looks out to the hills and there is a wide uninterrupted view, which, good as it is, does not include Fair Head.

Many of the usual people are here and we saw some of them at church this morning. We miss some of those who are not here — the Higginsons and the Daveys most of all. Jack can be met at every turn of the road, as he appeared in August 1940. When some people see Rab they will probably think of his owner who always had him close to him wherever he went.

We are looking forward to having you with us next Sunday. I have not looked up the trains yet, but I hope there is one that will suit you. We will look into it to-morrow and let you know. Last Sunday with you at Banbridge is a very happy memory. Unfortunately, you will not be able to stay here till nine o'clock in the morning.

I will likely have to go to Belfast once or twice in the month, if there is a cheap day for traveling: we have not found out yet if the excursion rate still prevails. I'll let you know so that we may meet if possible.

It does not seem long since you came to us in Ahmedabad. It was in the cool days of the monsoon, when there was a fresh breeze blowing in through the open windows and the *compound was covered with new and tender grass. It has been like that ever since. May it long continue to be so, and by the blessing of God upon you and all your work, hard though it may be, may your life bring rest and refreshment to many.*

Your loving D

PART THREE

My Family

1951–1975

The Lark in the Clear Air

Hello there. It's me, WH Junior, back telling this story. Now that Mum and Dad have introduced themselves, you may wonder how they first met. It's a shame that I don't know when and where this encounter took place, but I do have bits and pieces of their story.

In 1947 when Grandpa Boyd was appointed moderator, he chose Ray Davey and Dad as his two chaplains. Mum said that her father noticed Dad when his church in Randalstown, the Old Congregation, collected a record amount of funds for the Foreign Mission.

In 1950 Dad was called to be the new minister in Windsor, where the Boyds worshipped. Around that time Dad needed to buy a new pair of grey flannels. He went to a shop on the Falls Road, but found everything too expensive, until the tailor brought out a piece of material left over from making a suit for a VIP, Dr RH Boyd. Perhaps this purchase brought the two 'men of the cloth' together. Uncle Billy first met Dad when Mum invited him for a meal with her family in Osborne Park. Gran disapproved of young people going out together. It just wasn't done. This was the first time any of her children had invited a member of the opposite sex into the family home. Afterwards Grandpa said, with a twinkle in his eye, that had he known the consequences he would never have chosen William Hanna as his chaplain.

Grandpa gave the address at my parents' wedding on 28 June 1951. Windsor Presbyterian Church was packed. The organist played 'The Lark in the Clear Air', Dad's favourite Irish melody. The *Belfast News Letter* of the following day includes a photograph of the handsome couple, standing against a backdrop of the church, confidently facing the camera. Dad was dressed in a frock-coat. The bride, '*was in a trained gown of golden satin damask and the veil of tulle was held in place by a tiara of pearls… When leaving for the honeymoon, which will be spent motoring in Scotland, the bride was wearing a bottle-green tailored suit, with white hat and accessories to tone*'.

Golden Hair

I first appeared in the world, and in this story, on April Fool's Day 1955. What happened next is hazy and under-recorded. John, my elder brother by thirteen months, had two entire photo albums devoted to him as a baby. All I got were a few snapshots. From this scant evidence I deduce that I spent most of my time lying on my back in a cot facing the ceiling, or in a pram looking at the sky, unperturbed by occurrences around me. 'Can he kick?' asked Grandpa.

Important events were happening in the wider world. In 1956 the USSR invaded Hungary, and Britain and France tried to invade Egypt. The British Empire of my grandparents' generation was rapidly shrinking. In 1957 Ghana was one of the first British colonies in Africa to become independent. In Europe, countries that had been at war a few years earlier decided to join together. Six of them, strongly influenced by Christian Democrat parties, signed the Treaty of Rome, setting up the European Economic Community (EEC). Although Winston Churchill had called for a United States of Europe as early as 1948, Britain stayed outside the new institutions of European integration. Northern Ireland also remained on the periphery, a divided place. The local Prime Minister, Basil Brooke, once said, 'If we in Ulster allow Roman Catholics to work on our farms, we are traitors to Ulster'. The latest campaign of the Irish Republican Army (IRA) was snuffed out when internment – political imprisonment – was introduced on both sides of the border.

Grandpa died in October 1957, and just before that my memories begin, for I am aware of sitting on the floor, by his green armchair, looking up at a white-haired gentleman. Mum gave birth to my sister in January 1958. Anne Louise was six weeks premature and stayed in hospital in an incubator. I remember walking under the bed in the hospital ward.

Mum used to lean over my cot, or pram, with her hair flowing down. She grew it long and wore it in various styles. I liked when she brushed it back and fixed it in place with corrugated hairpins.

My parents were the most beautiful couple in the world. Dad was six foot tall, with grey-blue eyes, a generous mouth and wavy dark hair. Mum was five foot eight, with blue eyes, striking features and a high forehead. Her skin was ivory and freckled and could take no sun. She played the piano a little. In the evenings she allowed me to sit on the stool beside her, as her long polished nails clicked on the keys and she sang the evening hymn 'Jesus,

Tender Shepherd'. She was protecting me from the dark. Each night she came into our bedroom and we said our prayers, blessing all the family and all our relatives, and never forgetting the refugees.

I often told my parents that I loved them. In my mind I had a special relationship with both of them, despite the fact that Mum thought John was more handsome than me. He was taller, and darker, whereas that phrase about my early appearance, 'as yellow as a duck's bill', was often repeated. As a toddler I was so thin Mum said that I looked like one of the children emerging from the Belsen concentration camp.

John only started talking once he had me to converse with. We were both shy, but he was shyer. I had to take the lead when kindly old spinsters in the congregation engaged us in conversation.

'Now which of you is William, and which is John?'

'I'm William, and he is John.'

Mum ran the household at Windsor Manse like a hospital ward. She carried out the unpaid duties of a minister's wife, raised three children, dealt with emergencies, and held down a full-time job in the health service. It was she who managed the family finances. 'Your father was hopeless with money. He entered our marriage with a bank overdraft because he had bought such an expensive engagement ring', she would say, as she rolled the three diamonds round her finger. We would have struggled as a family on a Presbyterian minister's stipend. It was Mum's salary, and her ability to make ends meet, which kept us going and, in later years, made us feel quite well-off.

We had home help in Windsor Manse. Mrs Ferris, a smiling lady who wore an apron and suffered from asthma, did the ironing. Mrs Webb, 'a real character' from the Shankhill Road, cleaned. Miss Stewart, a quiet seamstress, who wore half-circle glasses on a string, came once a week. Sewing to mend and alter clothes was essential. For many years all my clothes were hand-me-downs.

Mum did all the cooking; Dad having mastered little more than the boiling of an egg. She baked biscuits – flapjacks, coffee-flavoured cookies, and fudge. She cooked quickly, sometimes preparing delicious meals, and occasionally dashing off something less edible. As you may have noticed, a quick temper lurked under her Christian upbringing, although her strongest swear word was 'Damn'. (Dad's strongest swear word was 'Murder', which I long considered to be mild, until I realised it was his version of the French *merde*.) Mum occasionally smacked us when we turned up our noses at one of her less successful dishes, but the usual punishment was to be sent away from table, and into the cold coalhouse, to reflect on the plight of the 'starving refugees'. Food could not be refused. I once had the courage to decline a slice of lemon cake, and I never heard the end of it. 'William doesn't like lemon cake', she would inform the room. In our family a 'lemon cake' became the code-word for a story that parents repeat in order to embarrass their children and put them in their place.

Dad was good at mathematics, but Mum was hopeless. He was able to solve most problems by algebra, whereas she let us tease her about not knowing all her times tables. She was never sure of seven eights or nine sevens. But she was full of common sense. As a nurse, she dealt with blood without flinching, unlike Dad, who passed on to me his tendency to faint, a gene I could gladly have done without. Mum wasn't in the least prudish. On holiday she would undress publicly on the beach, embarrassing us all. When the sex education documentary *Helga* came to Belfast it was previewed by city councillors. At the point where the heroine gave birth on screen, some of the dignitaries fainted and others walked out of the cinema in protest. Mum, who had been invited to give an opinion on whether the film was 'suitable' for Belfast, laughed at the faint-hearted and thought we should all see the film for its educational value.

In 1970 Mum surprised us by going to Queen's University for a year to obtain a diploma in education. This helped her progress in her nursing career, from being a sister tutor in the Lagan Valley Hospital to becoming a manager and teacher of management training. Although she studied Plato and Rousseau for her DipEd, she was happier reading historical romances, watching TV soaps, and professing not to understand complex concepts. But she was quick as a flash to understand people. She knew at once whether they were to be trusted or not and was always surrounded by loyal friends. My sister was named Anne Louise Janet, after three of Mum's closest nursing colleagues.

Mum wrote fast letters, which became more and more difficult to decipher as the years went by. I see her with a cheap biro in hand, dashing off quick thoughts on a blue airmail letter, pausing for a second's reflection, and scribbling again, writing to her aunts in America, or to Uncle Robin in India or Australia.

Like her father, Mum was impatient, quick to take decisions, and expected things to be done at once. As a child she once told her parents, 'Everyone is in my way', and the phrase stuck. At the end of our evening meal she would declare, 'Two charming gentlemen will now wash the dishes', and they did so immediately. Dad used to say to us, 'Boys, when the Mater says jump, you jump'. It wasn't a warning, just sound advice.

After Mum died in 2010, my wife Paola put together a photo album of her throughout her life. As I look through it, I ask myself how people should best be remembered. Why should someone who was once a tall smooth-skinned young girl, a beautiful bride, a confident young mother, be remembered as the frail old lady she became at the end of her life?

When she was eighty, Mum asked me to accompany her to see an old people's home, but after our inspection she decided she was not yet ready to go there. As we said our farewells at her gate, she wiped away a tear from her eyes, and gave me a silver locket. Two days later, after the long journey back to Dar es Salaam, where I was then posted, I opened the locket for the first time, and it took my breath away. Inside was a lock of Mum's hair, cut by her father when she was eighteen years old. The colour was unmistakable – pure gold.

The Quiet American

Dad was thirty-five when he married. He had been best man at weddings twelve times and had enjoyed what he called 'a long fore-noon'. By the time I was born, he was thirty-nine, his once thick wavy hair beginning to thin out. In 1959 he travelled to Canada and the USA on a three-month preaching tour. He sailed away by ocean liner, leaving from Cobh harbour, like so many Irish emigrants in the past. In America he stayed with church families and was treated as a celebrity, preaching in front of large congregations in Pittsburgh and Michigan. Mum was left to cope on her own with three small children. For some of the time we stayed in a big house near the Margy Bridge in Ballycastle. A barking black dog terrorised John and me, and we clung on for safety to each side of our mother's skirts.

At long last Dad returned from America, wearing a

deep suntan and looking like a Hollywood movie star. I walked around his legs and under the table in the dining room. He brought us penknives given to him by the father of film star James Stewart, who owned a hardware store in Philadelphia and had attended one of Dad's services. He told us the names of the cars he had seen, Cadillacs and Chevrolets, Oldsmobiles and Pontiacs, and how he had climbed the highest building in the world, the Empire State Building. He had fallen in love with America, its vast novelty, and the openness and friendliness of the American people. They, in turn, seem to have fallen for the young Irish preacher, his conversation, and gift of the gab. He made lifelong friendships and wrote Christmas letters every year to all the people who looked after him in 1959. He returned to the United States with my mother in 1976, the bicentenary of independence, and stayed in Kalamazoo, a name he loved to roll off his tongue.

When we were children, America was a special place. My favourite TV shows were *Davy Crockett: King of the Wild Frontier* and *The Lone Ranger*. I named my first bike 'Silver' after the Lone Ranger's horse.

On a Friday evening in November 1963 we were in the Church Lecture Hall at a Cub Scouts meeting when we heard the news that President John F Kennedy had been assassinated. We watched the images of the open-topped car on our black and white TV. JFK was young and handsome, a war hero and an Irish American. It felt like our own leader had been murdered.

Dad promised that he would take John and me to America when we were older and had passed our 'Junior' exams. The 'Junior' was eventually replaced by O levels, and by the time we sat the exams America was in the midst of the Vietnam war and had lost some of its appeal. I was more interested in exploring Europe, and it was many years before I first visited the USA. Judy Collins' song 'My Father' evokes for me the magic of a father's promise, and the sadness that it was never fulfilled.

I suppose most boys hero-worship their father, at least to some extent. For me the worship was total, a religious adoration, celebrated every week. My father was a God-like figure. Each Sunday he appeared in church, dressed in black silk robes, with a blue hood and two white Geneva bands, and stood in the pulpit, high above the congregation, to lead the morning worship. Our pew was right at the front, under his gaze. We sat there politely, in our Sunday suits, and looked up to him as he talked about 'the Father, Son and Holy Spirit'. He was obviously the father, and I was his son. I never quite understood the notion of the Holy Spirit – some sort of invisible glue that bound us together.

I believed that I was special for my father because he gave me his Christian name. John was called after Uncle Jack. Because I was the one called William, the ladies of the church thought that I was the elder, and would ask me, not John, if I was going to become a minister like my father.

Dad had a commanding presence up in his pulpit, but at heart he was a shy person who overcame his natural disposition by hard graft, creating and adopting a persona – a holy one, or a serious one, or when neither of these was suitable, a comic one. The deep lines on his forehead became even deeper when he laughed. And boy could he laugh. He thought the simplest comic on the TV was hilarious. Slapstick humour would make him double up with tears in his eyes. It was infectious and soon we would all be laughing.

I only remember one occasion when Dad lost his temper. John and I were in the back seat of the car, in the hills above Dundrod, and we must have been playing up. Dad suddenly guldered 'Shut up'. We sat in stunned silence. We had never heard him raise his voice before, and we never heard it again. When I scarred the mantelpiece in the morning room, by running my toy Dinky cars up and down the varnished wood, I expected Dad to be angry. Instead he stayed silent and made me sit and watch the workman repair the damage – which never completely disappeared.

While on Sundays Dad played the clergyman, on Saturdays he was a passionate rugbyman. He was proud that he had founded a new rugby club at Randalstown. He would be pleased to know that today a Randalstown rugby jersey is displayed at the Ravenhill ground, the home of Ulster rugby.

When John and I were eight or nine, Dad would take us, on winter Saturday afternoons, to watch rugby matches at the CIYMS ground (Church of Ireland Young Men's Society), a couple of miles away, across the Lagan. He had captained the CIYMS team in the 1940s and enjoyed meeting old pals on the touchline and shouting his encouragement to the young men on the pitch. 'C'mon, boys. Come on, CI. You can do it. Let's see you now. Come on, drive, boys, that's the way.' When the whistle blew for the end of the match he took us into the dressing room and we stood by his side in our matching duffle coats, as he congratulated or commiserated with the half-naked players. When we left for home Dad didn't slow his pace for us. We had to run beside him to keep up.

In January 1964 Dad took us to see Ulster play the New Zealand All Blacks, the most famous rugby team in the world. We walked the whole way, up Derryvolgie Avenue, across the Malone Road, over the Kings Bridge, through Sunnyside, to the Ormeau and the Ravenhill Roads.

That afternoon the All Blacks' full back, Don Clarke, kicked a goal from the halfway line, an amazing feat to accomplish with an old leather ball that gathered moisture like a sponge. Clarke first dug a little mound with his heel, then set up the ball on top of the mud, with the oval end pointing forwards to the goal, and struck it with his toe. As it sailed over the crossbar, Dad said, 'You will never see a finer kick'. Dad made us leave the match early, fearing that his boys might get caught in the crush between the war memorial and the turnstiles. We headed home in the winter's evening gloom, walking together towards the Black Mountain, accompanied by the murmuration of starlings roosting on the bare trees of Belfast.

It was rugby that later brought me to Dublin, to watch Ireland play Wales. When I cheered for the men in green I first became aware of my Irish identity. But before that there was another fundamental question of identity awaiting me nearer home.

The Windsor Question

One day, when I was six years old, walking along Windsor Avenue by myself, I was stopped by two bigger boys who asked if I was a Protestant or a Catholic. I did not know the answer to the question, nor which response was the better one to give. I was scared and thought they were going to beat me up. What was I to say?

Ten years later many people in Northern Ireland were singled out and murdered just because they were thought or known to be Protestants or Catholics.

As a child, I was soon to learn about Protestants and Catholics, and other labels such as Unionist, Loyalist, Nationalist and Republican. Northern Irish people have their own understanding of these terms, but other readers may be confused. So, I shall digress for a moment and try to explain some of the political terminology we use in our part of the world.

When the conflict in Northern Ireland erupted it was not essentially about religion. We weren't all fighting over points of religious doctrine, although some fundamentalists would have had us do so. It was more a quarrel between two tribes, identified by religious labels, or simply by colours – orange and green.

However, that is not to say that religion didn't matter. It did. In the 1960s, when most people in Northern Ireland still attended church, religious leaders were powerful, and religious affiliation marked our divisions clearly. Nowhere was this more apparent than on Derryvolgie Avenue, where our Windsor Presbyterian Church stood at one end, and the Catholic Church of St Brigid's at the other. Protestants and Catholics worshipped in separate places and were sent to different schools. As a result, we didn't know one another. It had been different for my father, growing up in a mixed rural community in North Antrim, with many Catholic friends. The first time I got to know a Catholic was when I left Belfast at the age of 18.

There has always been disagreement on how the country should be run and who should govern it. The fundamental question was — and still is — should Northern Ireland continue to be part of the UK, or should it become part of a united Ireland?

Protestants were in the majority in the 1960s — around 60% of the population — and they controlled the Northern Irish Government, based in Stormont, on the outskirts of Belfast. Most of them, but not all, supported the union with Great Britain. Catholics, in the minority, generally aspired to a united Ireland. So Protestants were mainly Unionists and Catholics were mainly Nationalists. The more radical Unionists, prepared to march and even take up arms to defend their views, called themselves Loyalists, and the more radical Nationalists, similarly inclined, identified as Republicans. But there were always exceptions to such generalisations. Historically, leading republican figures such as Wolfe Tone, or Roger Casement (who I recently discovered was a distant relative on my mother's side), were Protestants. Some Catholics have always supported the union with Great Britain. And there were small political parties which tried to carry on politics without religious affiliation. But it was not easy to avoid being defined by either a Protestant or Catholic label. The joke was that Jews would have to explain whether they were 'Protestant Jews' or 'Catholic Jews'.

The question I was asked by the boys who stopped me on Windsor Avenue was not so much about religion as about identity. Which side are you on? Are you one of us, or one of them? I do not remember how I replied at the time, but I somehow managed to escape the interrogation unscathed.

Narrow definitions of identity have always been central to the Northern Irish question, and they are at the heart of conflicts all over the world. I believe that we all have multiple identities, and when we embrace diversity in ourselves and in others, the difficulties between us begin to disappear. That is why the motto of the European Union — 'United in Diversity' — has always appealed to me. Everyone is included.

Most people in Northern Ireland are decent, friendly and law abiding, but there have always been politicians who have sought power by magnifying differences between citizens, re-igniting fears and exploiting opportunities for conflict. This phenomenon is not, of course, limited to Northern Ireland. It is one which is seen more and more in today's Europe and America, as elsewhere in the world. Perhaps lessons from the Northern Ireland peace process may have wider relevance.

One final remark before we continue with the story. In this book I must choose words that are loaded in a Northern Irish context. I apologize if any reader is offended. Should Northern Ireland's second city be referred to as Londonderry or Derry? I have chosen Derry, because in the six years during which I lived nearby I never heard anyone call it anything else. Unionists who take exception to this will recall that most loyalist songs, including 'The Sash', refer to Derry. The words of these songs were drummed into me long ago.

The Twelfth

In his memoirs Dad writes of the magical change of seasons. The natural world meant less to us city-dwellers. Our year was marked by two special days – Christmas Day, when family gatherings converged on the manse, and the Twelfth of July, when 30,000 people walked right past our house in the largest and most exciting parade imaginable.

The lawns in front of the church slope down to the road, making the church grounds a natural grandstand – one of the best places on the Lisburn Road to view the parade. We children sat at the front by the wall where the church sold soft drinks and crisps to passers-by. Inside the grounds you could hire chairs and teas were served.

The day was always hot. It began in silence as traffic was halted on one of the busiest trunk roads in the country – the main road from Belfast to Dublin. We took our seats on the bench early and waited for ages for the first signs of the procession.

Around eleven o'clock, from far down the road at Tate's Avenue, came the opening salvo – the megaphones of the posse of preachers – religious fanatics, wearing sandwich boards bearing verses of scripture. They were an advance guard, walking from one side of the road to the other, urging the spectators to be 'saved'. 'The hour is nigh!' 'Eternity where?' 'JOHN 3:16' read the boards. One screaming red-faced man appeared year after year. He terrified us with his hectoring tone, but we always looked forward to his performance.

We knew these 'manic street preachers' were just the supporting act for the real thing – the Orange marchers and the bands. Gradually sounds began to reach us, faint and faraway at first, then in a crescendo of waves – a simultaneous medley of martial music. Brass bands, pipe bands, accordion and flute bands all vied for our attention. I can hear them now, all playing at once, or taking it in turns to opt out and listen to a single drum beat for a hundred yards or so before striking up again. The bands were separated by banners and companies of marching men, dressed in dark suits, bowler hats, brown shoes and orange sashes. Some office-bearers wore white gloves and carried swords that glinted in the sun. Hundreds of bands passed by the church, and we clapped for each one – staid applause for the elegant brass bands, enthusiastic cheers for the pipe bands, many visiting from Scotland, and wild whoops of joy for the flute bands. Oh, these were the greatest fun. Their tunes were well worn and catchy. At the head of each band youths and young boys twirled and tossed red, white and blue tasselled sticks higher and higher in the air, catching them as they came down, sometimes behind their backs, without even looking. The boys swaggered, jolly and carefree, from side to side across the road. Keeping them company along the pavement came girls in short skirts, wearing make-up and hats saying 'Kiss me Quick', dancing to the beat of the drums, singing in the strongest Belfast accents, always with an eye on the band leaders.

The giant colourful banners, one for every lodge, depicted different events. Some showed King William on a white charger at the Battle of the Boyne. Others were scenes from the First World War Battle of the Somme, and yet others were giant pictures of Bibles or biblical events.

The Orange parade took hours to pass us by on its way to the field at Finaghy. In the afternoon it returned with fewer marchers. By then the Orangemen had walked far and listened to speeches and sermons. Older fellows were allowed to ride in black limousines, from which they waved at us like royalty. Some, according to my father, might be 'the worse for wear'. The return march was less impressive, but still we watched and listened, wishing the day would never end.

As the sixties progressed and 'the Troubles' came upon us, we began to have doubts about the Twelfth of July, a celebration of a victory long ago by a Protestant king over a Catholic king. We were assured that Catholics also had their day to march in August with their Hibernian Society, but it was nothing so grand. In East Belfast and in Portadown, Orangemen chose to march through Catholic areas, knowing that they would provoke an angry reaction. Catholic friends fled Belfast on the day, intimidated and excluded. We grew up. We saw the divisions in our society and what caused them. By the time we were adults the day we had looked forward to as children had lost its appeal. My brother John was prompted to write to the paper in 1998:

> 'Many of us do it regularly on an individual basis — ignore our neighbour. But in these parts it often happens on a mass scale, and it is still happening in Portadown. To march triumphantly past your neighbour is ignoring him as best you can, given that you are on the same patch of ground. In my book this ignoring is about as far as you can get from loving of neighbours or enemies. As one who lives in a glass house, I will throw this stone.'

In my years of exile, in countries round the world, it has been the 17th March, St Patrick's Day, that I've celebrated, not the 12th July. When I left Ireland I found out how much I have in common with other Irishmen and women, wherever they come from on the island, and whatever their religious persuasion. On St Patrick's Day we can be united, not divided. We don't hate others because we think they are different. It's a day when we welcome people of all nationalities to be Irish too. Everyone wears green.

Nevertheless, the Twelfth has not entirely disappeared from my mind. Each year when the day comes around I recall my joy as a child, waiting for the manic street preachers to clear the way for the flute bands. My foot starts tapping and I begin to whistle familiar tunes.

These days I keep fit by running round an old horse

race-track in Brussels, or a rugby ground in Edinburgh. On the second lap, to pass the time and remember which lap I'm on, I start whistling tunes. Marching tunes work best. I have to admit that I start with an Orange medley – 'The Sash', 'Derry's Walls', and 'The Boyne Water'. When the band needs a break, to catch its breath, I count the drumbeats until there is a roll and the tune starts up once more.

Angels and Ghosts

It is long past bedtime. I am lying in bed, wide awake, looking up at the high ceiling. John, in the next bed, is fast asleep and breathing noisily through his mouth. John has asthma. My eyes turn towards the window and gaze through to the red neon sign of the nearby Majestic Cinema. That's where they will come from. I know they will. They always do.

Whoosh. Twin white lights enter the room, run along the top of the wall, pass over John's bed, veer sharp right at the corner, and race to the door, where they vanish, only to be replaced by new lights at the window. And more and more. There is no stopping them. 'John!' I call out. 'I'm scared.' But John sleeps on, as the angels and ghosts continue their nightly invasion of our bedroom.

I can't stay. I can't lie here waiting. There is only one thing to do – make a dash for it. Leave the safety of the bed, run to the door, grab the handle. I'm there. I'm safe, but only for a moment. Now I have to open the door and run the gauntlet of yet more ghosts down the landing. No turning back now. Twelve steps to my parents' door, and I've made it. Safe again. My mother is the lightest sleeper in the world. She says it's because she was a nurse during the War and had to do night duty. I call out her name. She is awake at once and lets me enter my parents' bedroom. 'Don't wriggle,' my father tells me, as I climb up into his side of the bed.

**

A winter Sunday evening. Starlings are roosting on the city's telephone wires. In the kitchen Mum prepares scrambled eggs on toast and puts the plate and a pot of tea on a tray. It is my job to carry the tea upstairs to Dad's 'busy room'. I climb the stairs, knock, open the door, and take the tray carefully over to my father, sitting at his desk in the middle of the room. It's an oak rolltop desk, gifted to him by his church in Randalstown. On it is placed the silver inkwell the rugby club awarded Dad in 1950. I place the tray on the desk and Dad pulls out one of the little secret tables, on the right side of the desk, for me to place my piece of toast on. A gas fire warms and lights up the room, white elements turning to orange and red under a blue flame. Dad takes a puff from his Peterson pipe, and clouds of smoke fill the room. With his Parker 51 ink pen between his finger and his thumb, he scratches some words of his evening sermon onto the jotter. The radio is on, playing Franklin Engelmann's *Down Your Way*. Sometimes we will listen to Alistair Cooke's *Letter from America*. When I'm bored, I play under the legs of the desk, around Dad's feet, or go to the bookshelves and quietly press all the books back against the wall and then forward again. Dad finishes his tea, wraps up his sermon, and I take the tray back to the kitchen. I will never be closer to my father than in his study on a winter's Sunday evening.

***

Ten years have passed. I no longer sleep in the same room as John. Dad's study has moved downstairs, and the room where I brought him Sunday tea has become my own bedroom. Come in and have a look. The carpet is turquoise, new and cheap. I feel the ridges under my bare feet. The curtains are lemon yellow. They allow sunlight to bathe the room in summer. Brigitte Bardot, in black and white, sits astride a Harley Davidson motorbike on the wall by the door. She faces my bed. Hanging on a peg on the door is my dressing gown, cheap silk in a Paisley pattern. Next to it I have nailed with tacks a cloth map of Manchuria, a memento from my grandfather's visit in 1936. Opposite is Miss Hamill's chest of drawers, dark-brown oak, its mirror permanently tilted upwards, a rust stain towards the bottom on the right. In this corner of the room I carry out my morning and evening exercises – press-ups and sit-ups. Lying on the chest of drawers is a pair of anthracite trousers, creased and shiny from hundreds of hours sitting on school benches. If I look down to the left I will see the tin wastepaper basket in a psychedelic 1970s design – green, purple, black and blue. Everything is in its place, in full colour: the mahogany wardrobe, lined inside with red and green wallpaper, the single bed with its rickety oak headboard, the maroon counterpane, the itchy green nylon sheets, the fluorescent maroon lamp, the wooden model ship on the mantelpiece, three teak Indian birds, my Bakelite radio (Athlone, Hilversum, Luxembourg...), the two-bar electric fire that attracts pieces of wool fluff. We may turn it on for ten minutes on winter mornings. Each object holds its place, undisturbed. I can go to any corner of the room and tell you exactly what it contains. My bedroom, first room of my own, filled with a unique assembly of familiar objects, is still there – half a century later.

Words and Music

When I was six years old I was a dreamer and loved to listen to our teacher Miss Lamont reading to us about faraway, magical places. I wrote a story of my own, six pages long. The exercise book was divided horizontally, blank at the top of each page, lined in the bottom half, so that you could illustrate your stories as you composed them. What did I write? Something inspired by Miss Lamont's story about a boy called David who had a magic carpet and could travel on it to anywhere in the world – places such as Turkey and Tibet, where yaks roamed about.

On holiday in Wales, when we couldn't fall asleep in the summer evenings, I would make up stories and tell them to John. He would ask for more. They had to do with acquiring precious things, and imaginary houses in different worlds. Telling these stories made me feel alive. It was as if, by making up stories, I really possessed all the riches and had visited all the exotic places I had conjured up.

From time to time Mum and Dad worried about my learning. One day they decided that I was not reading enough. They compelled me to sit down in Dad's study for ten minutes every evening after tea and read pages of a book by Arthur Ransome called *The Big Six*. I sat begruntled on the floor, putting in the time. I pretended to read five pages, when really my eyes were glued to one word.

CS Lewis's *Narnia* interested me more. Auntie Beth gave me a copy of *Prince Caspian* and I soon read the others. The children in CS Lewis stories seemed like me. They were dreamers, moody, sometimes naughty, intrigued by magical places. Lewis' *Narnia*, based on the scenery around Rostrevor in Co Down, spoke to me more than Ransome's English Lake District.

John and I soon made a more exciting discovery. The family spent a weekend in a hotel in Donegal town, where we boys shared a room. On the bed we found a Pan paperback of the first James Bond book, *Casino Royale*, left behind by a previous guest. We decided not to tell our parents. It didn't look quite like the books to be found around the manse. John read it first and passed it to me. We entered a world which grown-ups did not talk about, but which we had suspicions of – an adult world of spies, secret agents and sex. We used all our pocket money to acquire more of this powerful stuff – *Dr No*, *From Russia with Love*, *Goldfinger*, in which James Bond not only encountered the strangely named Pussy Galore, but also showed off his skills on the golf course, playing off a single-figure handicap, without ever needing to practise.

At school, in our extra elocution lessons, the blue-haired Miss Weir attempted to rid us of our Belfast vowels and spiky consonants, by making us read out loud the second chapter of *101 Dalmatians*, in which '*Cruella De Vil's dinnah pahty took place in a black mahble room and everything tasted of peppah*'. At home, in my private reading, I had discovered the second chapter of *On Her Majesty's Secret Service*, in which James Bond makes love to a girl he has just met, after overtaking her sports car on an alpine road. I memorised the dialogue. On the school trip to Portrush that marked the end of our preparatory education, I packed two James Bond paperbacks in my duffel bag – *Diamonds Are Forever* and *Thunderball* – and took them out to read on the train. Ivor Ferguson, our school master, discovered them. He blushed and appeared shocked – 'and you, a minister's son' – but did not confiscate my sinful entertainment.

From Bond we progressed to the war heroes of Alistair MacLean. I read all the Nevil Shute novels, while John explored DH Lawrence, whose *Lady Chatterley's Lover* had been banned until the 1960s. We both read Thomas Hardy, although Mum steered us away from *Jude the Obscure*, a novel her father forbade her to read, perhaps because the hero murders his children, but more likely, I think, because Jude loses his faith in God.

When I came across a Penguin list of the fifty best books in the world, my reading branched off in all directions. John read Flann O'Brien, enjoying his crazy humour and Irish magic realism. James Joyce should have been next, but John was loyal to O'Brien, or Myles na gCopaleen, another pseudonym of the lesser-known genius, born in Strabane, whose real name was Brian O'Nolan. John also enjoyed *The Life and Opinions of Tristram Shandy, Gentleman,* a book I finally got round to during lockdown.

As our literary tastes diverged slightly, so did our musical tastes. We were both Beatles fans, but John got into the heaviest *White Album,* whereas I stuck to the middle of *Abbey Road.* I bought the first LPs of a string of singer-songwriters – Elton John, Judy Collins, Joni Mitchell, Leonard Cohen, whereas John bought blues LPs. A friend introduced us to Taste, led by Rory Gallagher, the amazing blues guitarist from Cork. We saw him in concert at the Ulster Hall, and leapt up and down as he sang and played. We enjoyed Finbar and Eddy Furey who introduced us to the uilleann pipes. We listened to Bob Dylan's double album of *More Greatest Hits* often enough to wear out a few needles.

I went on to discover jazz, but John stuck with the blues – Muddy Waters, Sonny Terry and Brownie McGhee, Champion Jack Dupree, BB King and Elmore James, who he considered the greatest guitarist. 'Dust My Broom' was his favourite song. The blues seemed to match John's growing mood, his inner soul. John introduced me to Van Morrison with *St Dominic's Preview.* We shared Belfast's pride at producing a great rock artist, as outstanding in his field as footballer George Best was in his.

Ballybradden (ii)

Each year we spent a week of our Easter and summer holidays at Ballybradden, Loughgiel, the farm where Dad grew up, in the townland where the Hannas have lived for generations. Uncle Robbie, Dad's younger brother, had inherited the farm and had married Auntie Inita. We had four cousins of our own age to keep us company – Roy, Carmen, Christine and James. But a week was a long time to be away from home in Belfast, and I missed Mum and Dad. So did John, but he didn't say so. We were townies and were sent to the country to be toughened up.

When the whole week had gone by, and Saturday finally arrived, John and I walked to the end of the winding front lane, to the wooden pallet where two milk churns were placed for collection, and waited, not for the milk lorry, but for our parents' car to arrive from Belfast.

Inside the family homestead the downstairs ceilings

sagged under the weight of generations. The stairs, covered by a floral carpet, squeaked under each tramping descendant. Hanna men are broad-chested and heavily built, useful material for the front row of a scrum. Dad was a prop forward and my cousin Roy played as prop for the Ulster Schools XV. The worst of the sagging was in the living room, directly under the boys' bedroom. I was always looking up in fear that the ceiling would collapse on top of me.

Fortunately we were not often in the living room. Boys were supposed to stay outdoors, banished from the house all morning and afternoon, only allowed in for meals, or if the weather was atrocious. Next to the back door was a water tap with a black hose affixed to it. There Uncle Robbie stirred cold water into a bucket filled with meal, his bulky hand mixing the food for the young calves. I marvelled at his fingers – swollen to twice the size of my father's – thirty years of wielding farm implements and carrying sacks, compared to his older brother's thirty years of holding a pen and announcing the benediction. Once the meal was well mixed, Uncle Robbie lifted the pail with one arm, sticking out the other at right angles to keep balance, and walked down to the whitewashed out-house where the calves stood on a bed of dungy straw, steam rising from their hungry mouths, saliva dripping.

A wooden barrel in the yard collected rainwater off the corrugated roofs of an outhouse. Here James drowned the kittens, doing as his father told him, placing them in a sack tied up with a piece of hairy twine. Perhaps stones were placed in the bag to weigh it down. The porous jute allowed the water to seep into the bag and little bubbles to escape. Was there any sound?

In the 1960s, Ballybradden, like hundreds of other small holdings in Northern Ireland, was still a mixed farm, of just fifty arable acres, with some cattle, sheep, pigs and hens. Uncle Robbie had around fifteen sheep, and by Easter time the ewes had produced twenty to twenty-five lambs, small black-face brockies crossed with Border Leicester. I performed a ceremony to baptise the lambs. One called Nibbles survived to bear lambs of her own. We were never there on the day the lambs disappeared. We didn't dwell on the connection between our lovely woolly pets on the farm and the slab of juicy meat on our Sunday dinner table.

The byre was a dry-stone whitewashed building. In summer swallows built their mud nests in the eaves, flitting in and out. Motes of dust danced in the sunlight streaming through window-panes edged by cobwebs. The must of ages, a mixture of cow dung and swallow guano, hung on the air. An electric rumble signalled that the milking machinery had been switched on. Uncle Robbie sat on a three-legged stool, his head resting against the flank of the brindle cow. Early morning, and again in the evening, he began the milking by washing the cow's udders. He talked lowly to the cow: 'C'mon, ye girl. That's it, that's the way', coaxing her gently as he attached the red rubber ends of the pumping machine to each teat. The milk filling the aluminium churn was warm and frothy.

The girls, Carmen and Christine, were expected to cook and bake and help indoors. Like their mother they were musical, studied the piano seriously and passed all their grade exams. They owned a record player and, when we were allowed inside the house, we listened to the latest 45 records and LPs – Andy Stewart's 'A Scottish Soldier',

Frank Ifield's 'She Taught Me How to Yodel', and the Beatles' *Rubber Soul.*

Farm work was never ending, feeding different animals, moving them about, opening and closing gates, milking, lambing at Easter, mowing and harvesting in the summer. I never fathomed why we did what and in what order. I followed James around because he seemed to have a general idea. But even he often got things wrong. Uncle Robbie spoke strangely, with a strong Ulster Scots accent. We couldn't understand him. When he asked us to do something we kept saying 'Pardon?' He would speak louder, but it didn't help. Anne Louise seemed to be on his wavelength. They were closest of friends. He tickled her and teased her about her dimples.

There were always dogs around the farm, some friendlier than others. I once saw a corgi, edgy and unpredictable, bite a cow in the ankle and take it down. The same dog bit me in the hand, across the web between my thumb and forefinger. Rover, a working collie, was my favourite dog. He slept in an outhouse on a piece of sacking so that he wouldn't get spoiled. He understood Uncle Robbie's whistled commands. One day it was my turn to bring the cows in from the field, with only Rover to help. The cows stood around the rutted entrance to the field, reluctant to pass through the open gate, wondering if they might disobey such an obvious townie. I gesticulated wildly, while Rover looked up at me, waiting for the correct calls to be given. I remembered this incident many years later when an American ambassador, seeing me trying to persuade my European colleagues to all agree to a common position, told me that my job was like herding cattle.

On Sundays Uncle Robbie scrubbed up, dressed in his Sunday suit and drove us in the Hillman Sunbeam to Ballyweaney Presbyterian Church. The packed congregation sat silently in their pews, regarding one another, on the lookout for novelties to be whispered about and commented on later, such as haircuts or new hats, until the organ began softly. Uncle Robbie sat at the end of the family pew, upright and shaven, red-cheeked and balding, a strong and silent Ulster farmer, elder of the church, observing the Sabbath day. The days of his farm were numbered, like so many other Ulster small farms. In the sixties there was no cash crop to replace the flax that had funded my father's education. Farms had to be amalgamated, not divided between brothers, as Ballybradden had been a generation ago. Did Uncle Robbie have an inkling that his years of toil, of back-breaking work, would provoke a heart attack at the age of fifty, that his sons would shun farming and escape to England, and that, when he died, the farm he had inherited, which had been in the Hanna family for centuries, would be sold to the family next door?

A Foreign Country

I read in the *Belfast Telegraph* recently that a Northern Irish politician was complaining, with a great dollop of indignation, about the EU and the Northern Ireland Protocol. She referred to the Republic of Ireland as 'a foreign country'.

Perhaps many years ago we did think of the Republic as foreign, but not in a threatening sense – we were always charmed by the place. We spent many summer holidays there and I always associated the Republic of Ireland with beaches and freedom and the joy of being elsewhere.

There was a first July, long, long ago, that we spent in Blackrock, just south of Dublin. We were tiny then and wore knitted swimming costumes. John walked across the sand ridges at low tide, all the way out until he was a dot on the distant margin of the Irish Sea. In Waterford we stayed in a Christian holiday home, went out to sea in a fishing-boat and caught seventy-six mackerel off Tramore. At the end of our stay Mum embarrassed me by insisting that I join her in singing a duet party piece, 'There's a Hole in My Bucket'. We went on to Skibbereen and Barley Cove, where we stayed in a house where fluffy yellow chickens ran around the kitchen. There was neither electricity, nor enough beds. I slept in a chair and was lent a bicycle lamp to see by.

In the 1960s we spent several summer holidays at Rossnowlagh in County Donegal, staying in one of Mr Vaughan's caravans. We were sent out to play golf all day long on the little nine-hole course that used to nestle in the dunes, and sadly has now disappeared. On that springy turf, where you could lose a ball amid the daisies, I first learnt to love the game. I still go to Rossnowlagh in my head when I want to conjure up the feel and sound of a perfect golf shot. Jim Reeves' 'I love you because' played on the café jukebox. Huge daddy-long-legs crept around the corners of the concrete shower huts. One day Mr Vaughan came to tie down all the caravans to withstand the force of Hurricane Anna, but no storm ever arrived.

At Dunfanaghy Golf course in 1969, the greens were protected by barbed wire to keep off the sheep. We stayed with cousins in Portnablagh, in the flat above Mullins the grocers, and listened on the radio as Neil Armstrong walked on the moon.

The next year we were in Connemara, playing tennis on a tarmacadam court beside a hotel in Clifden. Our cousin Roy was allowed to go out by himself to a local dance where, according to Dad, he might 'paint the town red', whatever that entailed. On the road to Clifden we stopped our car to help a man whose horse had collapsed under too heavy a load of turf. Dad was most concerned. He enquired, in his Country Antrim accent, how he might help, but the fellow didn't seem to understand what he was saying. He looked at Dad oddly and said, 'Do you have English, sir?'

And there was a glorious summer in Fermoy. On the way there we stopped off for a picnic by the River Shannon in Athlone. Mum and Dad smoked Sweet Afton cigarettes, *'to keep the flies away'*, according to Mum. A friendly road sweeper, learning that we had travelled all the way from Belfast, shook his head in amazement: 'Sure, all Ireland's on the move'.

I was fifteen and John was sixteen. One evening we went to the local ballroom and heard Ireland's top show band – Dickie Rock and the Miami – play cover versions of all the latest hits. At the dance John met a tall brown-haired girl from Mitchelstown called Peggy. I was happy for John, but also jealous, and had to walk home alone. John fell for Peggy, who liked him too. When we returned to Belfast he wrote to her and she sent him her picture. At the beginning of September, instead of going back to school, he set off hitch-hiking all the way across Ireland to see her. When John died a few years ago, among his few belongings I found a Polaroid picture of Peggy, sitting at the top of one of the hills above Fermoy, smiling and tossing back her brown hair.

In the South of Ireland the people spoke differently, and we mimicked their accents. Maybe they did inhabit a foreign country, but it was our own foreign country, a place that we fell in love with, and where we too belonged.

Cockles and Mussels

It's a bright and chilly Saturday morning, early in February. The sun is in Dad's eyes all the way, as he drives 100 miles south, from Belfast down to Dublin. Uncle Billy sits in the front, John and I in the back. Our bottle-green Cortina, registration no AIA 2910, winds through the main streets of each small town – Lisburn, Dromore, Banbridge, and Newry. We cross the border, marked by a wooden hut, with words painted in Irish. The road signs change from red, black and white to yellow and black. At Dundalk we stop for refreshments at a cinema café. It takes ages to pass through the winding streets of Drogheda and on to the high TV masts of Dublin.

It is the first time in the city for John and me, but Dad, proudly wearing his Trinity tie, knows the place well. He drives along O'Connell Street, past the GPO, which was attacked in the year of his birth, and the place where

Nelson's Column used to be before it was recently blown up. We park at St Stephen's Green, where a wee man guides us to a parking space and tips his hat when Dad gives him a shilling. We have lunch in the upstairs dining room of a white-painted hotel on the north side of the Green. Dark-haired waitresses, in black frocks and white pinafores, serve us ham and potatoes with white sauce. After tea and biscuits we set off on foot to cover the couple of miles to the international rugby ground at Lansdowne Road.

As we walk through the capital city, crowded pubs are spewing out drinkers, and we are soon accompanied by a mass of rugby supporters, joking and shouting, swelling into a throng that owns the road and brings motor-cars to a standstill. We pause for a train to pass the level crossing under the West Stand. 'Apples, pears and chocolate!' shout out the Dublin street-sellers, their accent piercing the air, like Molly Malone crying 'Cockles and Mussels'.

Through contacts in Ulster rugby circles, Dad has procured four touchline seats. We take our places on the second row of three wooden benches placed on the grass. This is not a great vantage point for youngsters when the action is far away, but when the ball comes over to us we are close up to all our favourite players, all our heroes. Today Ireland, led by Tom Kieran from Cork, is playing Wales, led by Alun Pask. A Welsh placard showing a Tiger-striped forward says 'Put a Pask in your Pack', echoing the latest advert for ESSO Petrol 'Put a Tiger in your Tank'. There are five Ulstermen on the Irish team – Roger Young and Mike Gibson at half back, Ken Kennedy, Willie John McBride and Ronnie Lamont in the pack. Lamont is an old Instonian, and we have already seen him playing for my school's Old

Boys' team at Stockman's Lane in Belfast. The programme informs us of the size and weight of each player, as well as his profession – dentist, solicitor, doctor, or bank manager. Rugby is still an amateur game, played by professional men.

The teams line up far across the pitch, Ireland in green and Wales in red, and we stand for the anthems. The Welsh sing 'Land of My Fathers' in Welsh, so beautiful and stirring that it brings tears to the eyes, even of the Irish fans. Next comes our anthem, which Dad tells me is called 'The Soldier's Song'. We Ulstermen stand to attention, but our lips are sealed, because the anthem is in Irish and we don't know any. It's not as powerful a song as the Welsh, but it goes pleasantly this way and that, climaxing with cheers of 'Ireland', 'Ireland', which we can finally join in. Few people seem to know all the words, but it's a rousing tune all the same.

***

On that chilly February day in 1966, after our team won the match, we returned home to Belfast, with our minds filled with images of our green-shirted heroes. The next year we had better seats, in the West Stand, and witnessed the elegant English back line in full flow – Duckham, Spencer, and Webb. After Duckham ran in a try from 60 yards, a lady beside us, dressed in a fur coat, commiserated with my father in a posh Dublin accent and passed him a bottle of whiskey, which he politely declined. It was a friendly gesture, if misdirected to a teetotalling clergyman. I had a sense of pride, of us all, Northerners and Southerners, being in the same boat.

'Ah, to be sure, it was a well-taken try.'

'Och, it was indeed.'

Since those days of watching Ireland play rugby football, with some of the finest players hailing from Ulster, I am filled with pride when the Irish rugby team play well. In the past we often suffered defeats, which John and I felt keenly, but today the Irish rugby team is one of the best in the world. We also have a single team in cricket, which has been fairly successful in recent years. However, Ireland continues to field two teams in association football. I recently walked past Windsor Park in Belfast, half an hour before an international match, and saw all the Northern Irish fans wearing their green shirts. Wouldn't it be great if we could field a single soccer team and have a chance at World Cup glory?

Climb Every Mountain

Ruth was the first, and the prettiest, but I don't remember much about her. She came from Wädenswil near Zurich and was the niece of my mother's Swiss governess. She had long dark hair and was just seventeen years old. Her room was directly above mine, in the attic on the top floor of the manse. There she had a record player and allowed me to sit on her bed and listen to 45 records playing over and over again.

There was 'Telstar', an instrumental, Nina and Frederick's Christmas song 'Little Donkey', and my favourite, 'Venus in Blue Jeans'. 'Venus' was a hit in 1962 for Mark Wynter, who covered the US version of the two-minute song, complete with false American accent. It reached number four in the UK charts. This was just a year before the Beatles broke through, with their raw Liverpool sound: sugary pop songs, sung by boys with brushed back hair, were still all the rage.

My mother later told me that poor Ruth was very homesick. She found a local boyfriend who kept her out late. One Saturday night they had to throw gravel at my parents' window to wake them up to open the manse doors.

Evelien was our second au pair girl and came from Amsterdam. She was with us for the 1962/3 winter when the snow lay deep. In early February only seven of our class managed to trudge through the drifts to turn up at school. Our teacher Miss Strahan, in her pleated tweed skirts and long boots, also made it through the snow to Inchmarlo.

Evelien was friendly and direct and spoke English well, in the Dutch manner. She enrolled at Queen's University, studying classics as well as English. She was older than Ruth, turning nineteen during her year with us. She already knew a thing or two about life.

We were standing in the kitchen one cold dark evening. John and I were drying the dishes. The work surfaces were covered with red plastified paper to match the red and black-flecked linoleum floor. The cupboards had recently been repainted dark blue. On the wall the red minute hand of a convex electric clock swept silently. I think Mum was also in the kitchen when I asked how babies are made.

It was Evelien who replied and who explained in detail. I wonder now what words she used for private parts of the body, because these were never named in the manse. I felt the blood flowing to my ears, but Evelien did not seem in the least embarrassed. Did my father do that with my mother? It was unimaginable.

In 1963, when the summer finally came, we travelled by boat from Larne to Stranraer, and by car on to Haddington, just south of Edinburgh. Dad had an exchange with the minister there, Joe Ritchie, swapping cars, manses and church services. It wasn't much of a holiday for him, for in the middle of it he had to return to Belfast when the church treasurer suddenly died.

Silvia was the last of our three au pair girls. She came from St Gallen in Switzerland, a city founded by an Irish monk from Bangor, Co Down. Her language was Schweizerdeutsch, and she sang in our church choir. She took a great notion to our cousins in Ballybradden and in Armoy and knitted dolls for them. Silvia was a cheerful girl with short hair. In my mind she merges into Julie Andrews in *The Sound of Music* – competent, encouraging, singing. I got on with her well. As for *The Sound of Music*, I had to go to see the film twice because, the first time, I walked out at the intermission, thinking the movie was over. It was a long film. It amazes me now to think of my parents allowing me to go to see a film, twice, in the centre of Belfast, all by myself.

That summer Dad had arranged another pulpit exchange, this time in Wales, in Llandinam, Montgomeryshire. The pretty little village took part in tidy-town competitions and there wasn't much for youngsters to do there. One day my parents decided that we would split up into three groups: each would go on a separate adventure, setting off in different directions. Dad was to go with Anne Louise, John with Mum, and I would set out with Silvia.

At the end of the day we reported back on how our trips had been. Dad and Andy, as we called her, had not gone far. Their route took them down to the River Severn, which was difficult to cross. They spent some time by the riverbank, before returning for lunch. Mum and John had done a little better, but had reached a busy main road, which prevented them from going further afield. They returned in the early afternoon. Silvia and I, however, had travelled far and wide. With a knapsack on her back, she led me up across fields and over stiles to the top of the Montgomery hills, and down again into another countryside. She reckoned we had covered all of ten miles to Newtown, where, exhausted and exhilarated by our adventure, we hitched a ride home.

The hike with Silvia was the highlight of my life so far. I lay awake that night, and on other nights, reliving the day. Today, looking back on that summer day in mid-Wales, my memory is sadder, for I see in those expeditions the destinies of our family. Dad and Andy, always close partners, gathered at the river far too soon, in the early 1980s. John and Mum struggled on, but their lives in later years were diminished by loss and illness. I was the lucky one, the boy who had the good fortune to step out, with a partner by his side, to climb mountains and travel the wide world over.

Ein Aber Bitte

Silvia brought her sixteen-year-old brother to stay with us in Northern Ireland and we got on well, riding our bicycles all over County Down. It was decided that the next year our whole family would stay with her family in Switzerland. This would be my first visit to Europe. We were to spend three weeks with Silvia's family in St Gallen, stopping off to see London on the way.

On previous trips to Britain we went by boat, but this time we took an aeroplane, my first flight. It was a BEA Viscount. We took off from Nutts Corner airport, later to be replaced by Aldergrove International Airport. Rabbits lined the runway. A stewardess handed us plastic cutlery and food. I spotted Bruce Tulloch, a well-known distance runner, seated a few rows forward in the plane. Silvia had given me an autograph book for my birthday. I was too shy to approach the athlete, but Dad was delighted to obtain his autograph for me.

In London, Dad, John and I stayed at the YMCA on Tottenham Court Road. Peering out of our room, down to the pavement below, I saw bright red lights and people standing around. Mum and Anne Louise stayed with relatives, in a grander part of the city, Sloane Square. Her cousin Angela was married to a doctor who ran each morning with Roger Bannister, the first man to run a four-minute mile. Mum obtained that autograph for me.

Dad was keen to take us to a BBC TV show, but all that was available was a radio programme, featuring 1930s band music, called *Those Were the Days*. At one point the host came over to ask us where we were from. Dad said County Antrim, not Belfast. Dad was in his element listening to the music he had grown up with, but we had developed more sophisticated tastes – the Beatles, the Rolling Stones and the Beach Boys, and were underwhelmed by our outing to the BBC. The event was not popular. There were so few of us in the audience that we had to gather close round the hanging microphones and clap as loudly as possible when we were given a sign. We visited Greenwich and saw the *Cutty Sark*. I ate too much at a Lyons' Corner House – it was the first time I had been to a self-service restaurant, and I took one of everything. I was sick at Heathrow after tasting cider at Uncle Alec's house. I was so ashamed that I hid away in a toilet where my parents couldn't find me, and we almost missed the plane.

Our second plane – a Vanguard – arrived in Zurich late at night. Silvia's family had ordered and paid for a taxi to take us all the way from Zurich to St Gallen, a distance of fifty miles. My parents were touched by this generosity. Silvia's teenage brothers were ejected from their bedrooms to make way for us. Her parents spoke no English but put up our family of five in their small terrace house on Rosenfeldweg. They introduced us to black cherries. Each evening we had bottles of *apfelsaft* with our meal – home-made apple juice fetched from the cellar.

Everything in Switzerland was more beautiful, cleaner and more wonderful than in Northern Ireland, and even than in London. It was warmer. The mountains were higher. The church was more modern. We travelled all around the country by trains that ran on time. Well-dressed ticket inspectors greeted us politely and cut holes of different shapes to validate our cardboard tickets. We visited Bern, beautiful and quaint in the summer evening, and Geneva, where my father dragged us along to see the memorial to the leaders of the Reformation.

As we crossed the bridge over Lake Geneva on a stifling hot day, a smiling photographer asked to take our picture. He promised to post the photos to Northern Ireland. Dad was happy enough to entrust him with his money, although Mum was unsure that the photos would ever arrive. They did, and they well record the visit of a Northern Irish family to the Continent in July. Look at the clothes! John and I are wearing Aran pullovers over shorts; Mum is uncomfortable in her suit and stockings. Dad, who has just bought an English paper and learnt of the resignation of Sir Alec Douglas-Home, the conservative Prime Minister, is wearing what he considered informal wear – jacket, tie, overcoat, and a rolled umbrella.

I too had a camera, gifted to me by American cousins Joe and Kay Taylor. I took photos, many out of focus or with a brown thumbprint in the corner, of St Gallen and its open outdoor swimming pool. When my film was finished Mum told me to take it to the chemist and ask for one more like it: '*Ein aber bitte*'. The three German words worked. Without any hesitation or request for clarification the shopkeeper gave me a new film. This was my first successful transaction in a foreign language.

As the train pulled out from St Gallen station, at the end of our holiday, we waved goodbye to Silvia's family standing on the platform and all felt sad to leave. It had been the best holiday of our lives, not just because of the beauty and wonders of Switzerland, but because the Gerosa family had been so kind to us. Mum pointed out a tear in Dad's eye. I didn't know that fathers could cry. I had thought that people only cried when something was wrong. It was the only time I ever saw him shed a tear. A tear for kindness.

La Gloire de Mon Père

In the summer months of the mid-1960s we were mad about cricket. On holiday in Wales we played in the evenings until eleven o'clock. When the tennis ball was lost in the garden next door we played on with a golf ball. At school our English headmaster, Edgar Lockett, taught us how to bat – forward-defensive or backward-defensive. I followed the English team – for at that time Ireland was not known as a cricket country. John supported the West Indies. During the long holidays we would wait for the Test cricket to start on the BBC at 11 am. There was no children's TV before then. I copied down the names of the English eleven: Boycott, Edrich, Dexter, Barrington, Graveney, Parkes, Parfitt, Higgs, Truman, Snow and Titmus – and noted down their scores.

In our final year at Inchmarlo, a special cricket bat was awarded to the most promising player. I desperately wanted to win it and was disappointed when it was presented to another boy. I had thought I stood a chance when I was chosen as captain for one of our matches – against Regent House in Newtownards. My father's younger brother Sam was a teacher there and everyone knew of him. My duties included making a short speech after the game to thank the mothers for making delicious sandwiches, and to congratulate the opposing team on their performance.

The cricketing highlight of the year, and of all our time at Inchmarlo, was the Fathers v Sons match, played on the pitch behind the preparatory school at Cranmore Park. Dad was in his late forties, older than most of the other fathers. He was a sportsman, of course, a fair golfer, but cricket was not his forte. He may have played on the beach with us, but I don't think he had ever before held a real cricket bat on a grass pitch, wearing pads to face a leather ball. Somehow he was selected for the Fathers' team, who batted first. One of their openers was Barry's father. He was a young man, a dashing player who walloped the ball all over the ground, made lots of runs for the Fathers, before retiring to give the Sons a chance. That was when Dad appeared.

My father walked on to the pitch wearing a pair of cream flannels he had purchased in the 1950s to play indoor badminton. I felt myself turning red. This was the 1960s and these were not the right clothes. Cricketers only wore white. When Dad arrived at the crease things got worse. He looked up at the umpire, not confidently as Barry's dad had done, but with the earnest smile that clergymen cultivate for tea-parties. He held his bat face forwards, rather than sideways as we all knew how to do, and asked the umpire for 'centre'. Not middle, not middle-and-leg, but centre.

The umpire smiled and assured him his guard was all right. I dreaded to think what was coming next.

Who was bowling to him? Perhaps Alan recalls, as he was our wicket-keeper. It might have been Gary, who had an elegant style, able to make the ball thwirl with spin through the air. Or maybe it was the other Alan, who had learnt his cricket in England. I was standing in my usual fielding position in the vicinity of short mid-on, where I sometimes managed to make a catch and sometimes did not. Dad faced his first ball. It bounced and reached him, and a miracle occurred. He connected with the ball cleanly, as he might hit a four-iron in golf. Wham, the red leather ball sped past me and banged emphatically against the brick wall boundary. Four runs.

Four runs with one blow. It was as well Dad did not have to run, as I'm not sure he would have known where to run to, or that he was supposed to cross with his partner. It did not matter to me that he was dismissed, clean bowled, with the next delivery, and had to make his way off the pitch so soon after his arrival. I no longer cared that he was dressed in creams or was older than the other dads. He could even have been wearing his clerical collar at the crease for all it mattered now. He had scored a boundary – with a clean stroke – and my prestige amongst my eleven-year-old schoolmates was secure.

***

I returned to Inchmarlo last year, with Tony, who shared my first years there. I looked for familiar objects in all the right places. The new headmistress had converted Miss

Kilpatrick's classroom into her office, and the blue-painted shaker cupboard where our lovely first teacher kept her sweetie jar had been removed. Outside the building I found the spot, by the bicycle shed, where, one day towards the end of my time at Inchmarlo, I stopped and said to myself, *this moment will never come back again*. Oddly, by taking a mental picture of that moment, I guaranteed that it would return again and again.

As I looked over to the green cricket pitch, today made of Astroturf, I could see Dad, sun-tanned and striding off the green field at Inchmarlo, the executor on one summer day, and for all time, of a single cover drive as sweet as any by Ted Dexter against the West Indies at Lords. '*La gloire de mon père*': My father in all his glory.

'We're Gonna Fix Yer Da'

One evening, when I was about twelve years old, the telephone rang in Dad's study. I heard the ring-tone and went into the room to answer. The study was a holy of holies, but I was allowed to enter in order to ask my father for help with mathematics, or to answer the phone if he was out. That evening Dad was at a committee meeting across the way in the church hall. Mum was also over at the church, leading a Women's Missionary Association meeting. Our parents had taught us to answer the phone. We were to answer politely, but not to reveal that they were out.

'Windsor Manse. Can I help you?'

'Is Reverend Hanna there, son?'

'I'm afraid he is not available at the moment. May I take a message for him?'

'You may indeed. Just tell yer Da that we are gonna fix him.'

The line went dead.

What did the message mean? It was clearly a threat. But how could anyone bear ill will to my father?

When I told my parents about the call they said that it must have been from the same people who had recently put up a sign on the lawn in front of the church saying: 'This church is going to Rome.'

The reason for the sign was not that my father had attended Mass or sprinkled holy water or indulged in some other Roman Catholic practice. However, he had recently introduced a joint Sunday evening service between our Presbyterian church and the nearby Methodist church, and had brought the time forward from 7 pm to 5 pm, in order to allow people to return home safely before dark. Just how this practical arrangement between two Protestant denominations was leading our church towards Rome has never been clear to me.

Nothing came of the threat to 'fix' my father that evening. But the same people who were opposed to the slightest change in religious practice were easily manipulated during those years by fundamentalist Protestant leaders. When I answered that phone call I began to come of age. I learnt that we lived in a deeply intolerant city, a place that was soon to be torn apart by hatred and violence.

Son of a Preacher Man

Dad never stopped working. All week he was at the church, at services and meetings, visiting the sick and writing sermons. He often took me with him in the car when he visited hospitals. I knew all the car parks at the City Hospital, the Royal and the Musgrave, where it seemed that the afternoon would never end. There was no waiting as long, no boredom as dull, as when I sat in the car wondering when Dad would come back from his hospital visit.

On Monday mornings Dad could have joined more relaxed clergymen friends for a round at Dunmurry Golf Club. He usually opted instead to make a start on his sermons. He would cross the Lisburn Road to the Windsor News Agency, and chat to Noel Baxter, the owner, whose face was scarred from a war wound. Dad would buy red notebooks, with blue-lined paper inside, pick up our copy of the *Observer* – in order to observe the Sabbath we read the Sunday papers on Monday – and *The Irish Times*, where he enjoyed the rugby reports by Van Esbeck. Back at the manse he would fill one of several pipes, with Mick McQuaid, Will's Walnut or Erinmore tobacco, and get down to the job of composing the message he would deliver to the faithful next Sunday morning. As the room clouded with wisps of smoke, he took apart the notebook, removing the staples, and wrote with his ink pen, first on one side and then on the back of the page. On Sunday, as he delivered the sermon, he would drop the sheets, silently, one by one onto the pulpit floor when he had finished, in a gesture that no one saw. His delivery was effortless. You never saw him reading or losing his place.

Mum said that Dad wasn't good at composing sermons when he first came to Windsor. So she helped him. On Saturday evenings, after tea, she disappeared into his study, and we were forbidden to interrupt them. Mum sat in a chair knitting, the needles clicking, as she listened to Dad reading his sermon to her. She said little but usually suggested he make it shorter.

Dad was a hoarder. He kept all his old sermons, sometimes recycling them when he was invited as a guest preacher in another church. He bound the pages up with a red ribbon, or a shoelace, and made a pile for each year, topped by a card with the date – 1961, 1962, 1963. He kept the bundles for many years, until after his retirement to a small bungalow in Carryduff, when Mum – who loved to clear things out – inveigled him into making a bonfire of the lot.

There were two services on Sunday, each requiring

a sermon. Dad's main work during the week went into the Sunday morning sermon. Among the congregation were a number of learned people – including various professors at Queen's University, who could be expected to follow the sermon critically and spot any flaws. For the evening service, with a smaller congregation, Dad was more relaxed. Since some people attended both services he had to prepare a different sermon, but he usually left the preparation until Sunday afternoon in his study upstairs.

When I became a teenager I began to wonder about the logic of Dad's sermons. Sometimes he chose a biblical text about one thing, and the story and moral lesson that followed were about something else. I also found that the better a preacher is at describing all that is wrong with the world, all the suffering going on, the more difficult it is for him to explain how God allows this to happen. Is God in charge or is He not? There is a tipping point in most sermons – you sometimes are aware of it and sometimes you miss it– where a little or large leap of faith is required. Around the same time I also found that *'Being good isn't always easy, no matter how hard you try'*. I tried hard to be good, and to believe, but somehow it didn't always work.

God Only Knows/
I'm a Believer

When puberty grabbed hold of me, around eleven or twelve, all I was interested in was girls. Because I attended a single-sex school, during the week I could only glimpse them from afar. A girls' choir from Victoria College once joined in a concert with us. I was the leader of the Inst boys' choir, and I thought the leader of the Victoria girls' choir was gorgeous. But I never had the chance to speak to her. Boys and girls were given no opportunity to mix.

Weekends were a better bet. Some girls played badminton on Saturday afternoons in the Lecture Hall. Between the games they ran around in short white skirts, giggled and whispered secrets together. Girls could also be seen close up at Bible Class on Sunday morning. I was an enthusiastic participant in David Bamford's class, never missing a chance to study religion in young female company.

The contest for my adolescent mind intensified with Crusaders. This was a group of Christians who met on Sunday afternoons. Unfortunately it was divided by gender. The boys had their group and the girls had theirs.

My parents didn't press us to join Crusaders. It was more a question of peer pressure. A few of the brighter boys at school and church attended the meetings, as did some talented sportsmen, including the McKibbin family, rugby internationals in successive generations. Since we were not allowed to play or watch TV on Sunday afternoons, Crusaders was better than sitting around in our bedrooms getting bored.

Crusaders had more modern music than at church, and the meetings were led by young enthusiastic leaders whose aim was to 'save' us. Becoming 'saved' was a specific event – a moment of conversion, when we were supposed to suddenly believe. I wanted hard to believe and be saved.

As well as Sunday afternoon meetings Crusaders held spiritual retreats to increase our opportunities of being saved. One such camp was held outside Bangor, and one at Rostrevor on the southern slopes of the Mountains of Mourne. During these weekends the assault on our young minds intensified. The leaders were sincere and convincing, and I was ready and listening to hear the call from God.

Gran and Mum had often read to us the Bible story of young Samuel who hears a voice in the night, and three times wakes up the old man Saul to tell him. On the third occasion Saul realises that the boy is hearing the Lord. I expected my call from God to be something like that. In Bangor I came close to persuading myself that I had heard a voice calling me. Each day I willed myself to have had the long-awaited spiritual experience, but the feeling died away. On the final afternoon at the Rostrevor retreat I was fooling around on a steep slope. I started to jump down and suddenly could not stop my fall. I sprained my ankle and felt stupid. The fatherly Crusader leader who bandaged my leg said to me that perhaps this fall was a message, a sign that I had been waiting for. I kept listening.

I do not recall how Crusaders disappeared from our lives. Perhaps we attended for three or four years – our adolescent years – but it never worked. Girls, on the other hand, did work. They were real. They danced, they looked our way, and I could hear their voices calling me. With girls, I was a believer.

When I was fifteen, the time came for me to take my first communion, along with other teenagers in the church. Dad held a preparatory class in his vestry and instructed a small group of us. Unlike the Crusaders he did not expect a sudden conversion. However he required something more. We all had to accept, and be willing to declare in church, that we believed in the Resurrection. We had to say the Creed, which declares that Christ died, descended into hell, and rose again from the dead. Accepting the Resurrection was the *sine qua non* to be admitted to take communion at church like other adults.

I attended all the classes. A lovely, dark-haired girl, wearing her Methodist College uniform, also attended, but I couldn't focus on her under Dad's gaze. There was no escaping the moment of truth.

To my mind then, and still today, there was a contradiction in my parents' approach to our education. They sent us to the Royal Belfast Academical Institution,

one of the best schools in the land, whose motto was
Quaerere verum: 'to seek the truth'. They urged us to
study and to think for ourselves during the week. But at
the weekend they expected us to suspend our reason and
believe that it was possible for someone to come back from
the dead.

What was I to do? If I confronted my parents with
my doubts I feared they would be disappointed in me. I
even thought that it could dent their faith. I spent nights
worrying about this, just as I later spent nights pondering
moral dilemmas in work. In the end I went along with it.
I decided to hope they might be right. Or maybe I just
copped out. Who can say? Maybe it was a bit of both.

Ten years later, when my daughter Luisa was born, we
travelled from Dublin to Donegal for Dad to baptise her.
Once more I had to stand before a church congregation and
answer a question about my beliefs. Again I put aside my
doubts and agreed to something my reason does not allow.
Later I had a dream that I was in St Johnston Presbyterian
Church, standing at the front with Paola. Dad had taken
baby Luisa in his arms, as he took so many children, and
enquired if I believed in the Resurrection. In my dream
instead of saying 'I do', I screamed, 'Dad I can't believe this,
I can't say it'.

The Big Man

Every five years, Uncle Robin returned to Northern Ireland on furlough from India. In 1961 he and his family – Aunt Frances, and our cousins Libby and Clare – stayed with us for the full year, occupying the top floor of the manse.

In 1969 Uncle Robin came alone to finish his PhD thesis. He stayed in the front room, the one from where a corner of the Windsor Park football ground was visible.

Since Uncle Robin's last visit things had been changing in Northern Ireland. In 1965 the Prime Minister, Captain Terence O'Neill, who came from the upper echelons of Ulster society and spoke with an English accent, had met his counterpart, the Irish Taoiseach, Seán Lemass, for talks. This worried extreme Protestants, fearful that their links to the United Kingdom might be weakened. In 1966, the 50th anniversary of the Dublin Easter Rising was celebrated by Nationalists who used the occasion to denounce the discrimination in jobs, housing and elections that they suffered under the Unionist government. In 1968 a civil rights movement emerged, inspired by black protests in the United States and student protests in France. Nationalists began to have new hope that their grievances would be answered. A civil rights march in Derry on 5 October 1968 was violently dispersed by police and this gained national and international attention.

Dad served on the Belfast Education and Library committee. He returned from one of his Friday morning meetings at the City Hall telling us how he had been impressed by a young student, Bernadette Devlin, who had argued the case for civil rights. The Clerk of Session of our church, Brian Rankin, a distinguished solicitor, was appointed to chair the Community Relations Commission. Leading members of our church knew that discrimination against Nationalists had to end. However, there were many within Presbyterianism who would not accept this and asserted that the civil rights movement was a 'republican plot' to be resisted. Disagreement over this caused tension within the Unionist community in Northern Ireland.

Civil rights protest marches met fierce opposition from Loyalists. On 4 January 1969 a march organized by Peoples Democracy students was attacked at Burntollet Bridge near Derry City and at least 100 people were injured. Rioting took place in Belfast and Derry. Police did not prevent loyalist extremists from attacking Catholics, particularly the most vulnerable, burning them out of their homes, as they had done in the 1920s. The army was brought in to patrol the streets of Derry and Belfast, and to keep Protestants and Catholics from killing one another.

One man stirred passions more than any other. Reverend Ian Paisley was a fiery preacher. He harked back to the Covenanters and 19th-century Presbyterian ministers, such as Roaring Hugh Hanna, whose statue occupied the centre of Carlisle Circus in Belfast, until it was blown up in 1970. Roaring Hugh Hanna was known for using thunderous oratory to whip a crowd into fury, to light the fuse that would cause them to riot and attack their neighbours.

We do not claim any relation to Roaring Hugh. Our family was at the opposite end of the spectrum of Presbyterian thinking. Our tradition was covenanting and evangelist, but it was also ecumenist. Our brand of Christianity centred on the second commandment to 'love your neighbour as yourself'. Ian Paisley, on the other hand, denounced the Pope as Satan, or the Antichrist, and was scathing about ecumenism. I could not understand how a person calling himself Christian could say such things. They were the exact opposite of what my father said and preached.

Ian Paisley first came to our attention when he protested loudly outside the Presbyterian General Assembly while it was debating leaving the World Council of Churches. He was not a Presbyterian himself, but he realised that Presbyterian church members could be persuaded to follow him, and when he set up his own church, he called it Free Presbyterian.

In the early days we viewed Ian Paisley as a figure of fun, like those Twelfth of July manic street preachers, bouncing up and down on his heels, working himself up into a self-righteous lather. We imitated his angry Northern Irish voice. But we underestimated how influential he could be, not only by directly attacking the Catholic Church, but also by denouncing as traitors any Protestants who showed religious or political tolerance. Paisley was a master in sowing division.

Uncle Billy was the minister of College Square Church in the centre of Belfast. He remembers how Ian Paisley condemned the flying of the Irish flag on the Falls Road and read out to the crowd the address they should attack. This led to a riot, and in the violence that followed, Uncle Billy's church was damaged.

Although Ian Paisley honed his skills as a clergyman, he soon became a politician. He was elected as an MP and later an MEP, forming his own party. We began to take him more seriously. One day Uncle Robin decided that he wanted to hear Paisley preach in his new church on the Ravenhill Road. He asked John and me to accompany him. He joked that we were to be his bodyguards.

We sat upstairs in the gallery of Martyrs' Memorial. The church was packed. We saw a different Paisley from the one we knew from the TV. In his own church, preaching to his followers, he was by turn light-hearted and joking, serious and devout. He was a showman, delighting in his role as an MP at Westminster, spending the first part of his sermon telling the congregation what he had said in Parliament the day before. 'I said to Jim Callaghan, I said, the People of Ulster will not surrender.' The congregation lapped it up. He ridiculed the Archbishop of Canterbury, naming him 'Old Red Socks'. Here was the amiable Big Man telling those people in London a few home truths. After giving his parliamentary report, Paisley shifted tone, and the service became a call for people to 'get out of their seats and confess the Lord as their Saviour'. And, of course, Paisley did not forget the question of money. He asked for 'a silent collection – I want to hear the rustle of notes, not the jingle of coins'. The congregation smiled and opened their wallets.

At this stage Uncle Robin decided that we should leave quietly, but we could not avoid the burly gentlemen holding out plastic buckets at all the exits. We had to pay for the privilege of hearing Ian Paisley preach.

In later years I sometimes imagined coming across Ian Paisley at the European Parliament, and rehearsed a speech in which I would tell him what I thought of him. Everything he found anathema – ecumenism, international cooperation, and the European Union – I found attractive. But the occasion to give the Big Man a piece of my mind never came. I did see him again one day, walking down the main street of Ballycastle, at the head of a procession of the Independent Orange Order, smiling and waving to the crowd. You would have thought him the mildest of men. It was always said of him that he treated his Catholic constituents as well as he did his Protestant ones.

Many Protestants, even though not adherents of his church, saw Paisley as a prophet. In the early years he kept saying that the IRA would rise again. This did happen and the IRA engaged in thirty years of violence, bombings and murders. But, as Ed Maloney shows in his biography, this was a self-fulfilling prophecy. For forty years Paisley not only attacked Catholicism but helped to bring down every Unionist leader who dared to move towards reconciliation and peace – Captain O'Neill, James Chichester-Clark, Brian Faulkner and David Trimble.

In the end Paisley seemed to have had a conversion to reason and common sense. In 2007, at the age of eighty-one, he took up the role of First Minister, against the wishes of his party and church. He sat down with the Deputy First Minister, Martin McGuinness, a former chief of staff of the IRA, and joked with him. It was astonishing. The pair of leaders became known as the 'Chuckle Brothers'. When Paisley offered visiting EU Commission President Barroso an Ulster Fry, McGuinness joked, 'He's trying to kill you.' Was this the same Ian Paisley whose watchword had been 'Ulster says NO'? He was old and ill. Did he have a moment of conversion, like Saul on the Road to Damascus, suddenly realising that, instead of persecuting people, he should turn around and love them? Did he fear what his maker would say to him on Judgement Day?

Maloney argues that Paisley was at heart a politician, an outsider who had worked his way to the top but had never been in power. Other leaders, such as John Hume and David Trimble, made peace and were awarded the Nobel Prize. In the end Paisley seized the opportunity of reaping the benefits of their work, to exercise power as the leader of Northern Ireland. It was too great a temptation for a politician to turn down.

Wearing the Right Collar

Soldiers arrived on the streets of Belfast in 1969. At first Catholics welcomed them as peacekeepers and gave them tea and sandwiches. On the Lisburn Road, we too welcomed these young men. They reminded Mum of her brother and his service as a young officer in the Indian Army. 'They could be Jack,' she said. The church rallied round. All day Friday, church ladies left packages behind the front door of the manse. In the evening a young officer called at the door, saluted us, and picked up boxes of cakes to be consumed back at the barracks. Different regiments had been sent to Belfast, but the most impressive, distinguished by their maroon berets and winged badges, were the men of the Parachute Regiment. Their young officer, with his public-school accent, was impeccably polite, as he thanked me for the cakes.

Mind you, these were real soldiers with real guns and

live ammunition. I will never forget the first day I heard gunfire across the city. It was strangely exhilarating. The Wild West had come to our town. It couldn't be real, but it was. One dark evening, when my father was returning from the church, soldiers stopped him at gunpoint and put him up against the manse wall. When he showed the soldiers his clerical collar, they let him go unharmed.

On 9 August 1971, internment was introduced. 340 men, all Catholics, were rounded up in West Belfast, detained without charge and some were treated brutally. No loyalist was interned, although much of the violence was being carried out by loyalist terrorists.

At school, the general opinion was that internment was a good thing. It would smash the IRA and peace would return. Uncle Robin held a different view. He told us that internment was the worst mistake the government could make. It would alienate Catholics and lead to more violence. He was right. Many innocent men were interned, some became active terrorists behind bars, and the anger that internment generated in the nationalist community provoked much of the violence that followed. This was the tipping point in a conflict that killed 3,500 people and injured 50,000 over the next twenty-five years.

In the confusion and rioting as internees were rounded up, we heard gunfire coming from across the Bog Meadows. We learned from the BBC that snipers had been shot by the army in Ballymurphy. I knew the Ballymurphy estate on Springfield Road. Earlier that year we had taken part in a community service project to repair a footpath there. When we heard about gunmen being shot, we hoped that would put an end to the conflict. There couldn't be that many IRA snipers out there, could there? The soldiers must have got them all.

In August 2021, fifty years after the events, the verdict in the inquest into the Ballymurphy killings was that the ten people shot dead during army operations were innocent, unarmed victims. Army officers had concocted the story about snipers that we heard and believed at the time. There were no reporters around to see what really happened. It took the relatives of the victims half a century to establish the innocence of their loved ones. One was a young priest, Father Hugh Mullan, gunned down as he went out, waving a white flag, to give last rites to a dying person. A clerical collar was no protection for Father Mullan; my father had been more fortunate.

Another Catholic priest, Father Edward Daly, was waving a white flag in Derry a few months later when members of the same regiment shot dead thirteen people taking part in a protest march against internment. That day, once more, I heard on BBC radio that the army had killed snipers. Next day on the wall facing our church in Belfast we saw freshly painted graffiti, as if celebrating a football match: Paras: 13; Bogside: 0. However, this time both local and international journalists saw what happened and reported. Even then it took two enquiries, the first of which was a cover up, and many years until the true picture of Bloody Sunday emerged.

As a sixteen-year-old, I did not realise that the army and BBC – pillars of the British establishment – could not be trusted to tell us the truth. It was only when I left Northern Ireland, on my first visit to France, that I found myself confronted with a critical view of my country and began to question my 'ancestral voices'.

Maintenant on parle français

We are midway across the Channel on our flight from Heathrow to Orly. We have spent three weeks together in Northern Ireland, where we spoke English. Now we are heading for three weeks in France, my first visit there. Nicolas, my exchange pal, decides he has had enough. It is time to turn the tables and switch to his language.

'*Voilà, ça suffit. Maintenant on parle français*'. Enough of that. Now we speak French.

My first French teacher at Inst pulled my hair at the temples and yelled at me when I made a mistake. Our next teacher was kinder, but uninspiring, and I learned little. Last year I was twenty-third in class, out of twenty-six, and Mum and Dad decided I needed private coaching. Kathleen, Ray Davey's wife, has been such a gifted teacher that my worst subject has now become my best. I am excited about visiting France for the first time and trying out the language properly. President De Gaulle, who used to shrug his shoulders and say '*Non*' to the UK's requests to join the Common Market, has been replaced by President Pompidou, who seems more likely to say '*Oui*'.

Nicolas' family is descended from Huguenots, the Protestant minority in France, and he is the son of a pastor of the French Reformed Church in Lyon, the third city of France. My mother's cousin John Higginson is the Director of the WHO Cancer Research Centre in Lyon. Kathleen Davey has found Nicolas through the Higginson connection.

Nicolas is seventeen, a year older than me. He wears glasses and is not interested in sport. He is an intellectual and a rebel, as many French teenagers are these days. In 1968 university and secondary school students in France protested and brought down the government of General De Gaulle. Nicolas and his friends are all politically aware. They wear short-sleeved crimson nylon shirts to show their socialist sympathies, whereas children of conservatives wear black shirts.

I don't think Nicolas has been over-impressed with his stay in Northern Ireland. We attended Ulster '71, a festival designed to promote Northern Ireland on the 50th anniversary of its foundation. But the concerts and cultural events have been overshadowed by the violence sweeping through the province. In February the first British soldier was killed. In March three off-duty Scottish soldiers were lured from a bar in Belfast and murdered. One of them was only seventeen years old. In June, hardline Protestants, led by the Orange Order, fought a pitched battle in Dungiven against the police and army, whose task it was to protect Catholics. It was courageous of Nicolas' parents to let him travel to such a crazy part of the world.

Nicolas and I hitch-hiked to Dublin, stayed for a couple of days in a bed and breakfast in Phibsboro, saw the violent western *Soldier Blue*, and ate a hamburger in a restaurant in O'Connell Street. Nicolas insisted on nicking the cutlery, something he assured me all French kids of his age do, as a matter of course. He sounded convincing, but I didn't join in the theft. Whatever would you do with stolen cutlery?

After Dublin we spent a week at a work camp at Corrymeela, in Ballycastle. Corrymeela was founded by Ray Davey in 1963 to be a centre of reconciliation between Protestants and Catholics. It is one of the few places where people from our two Northern Irish tribes can meet. Nicolas and I were supposed to meet young people from different religious backgrounds. We spent the days on the roof of one of the buildings, putting on new tiles.

For much of the week I lost sight of Nicolas, in his marine pullover and round spectacles. I was too excited by the prospect of nocturnal proximity between teenage boys and girls, and tried to get as close as possible to a girl from North Belfast who wore blue eye shadow. One evening we were on Ballycastle beach sitting around a campfire when she ran off. I chased after her and rugby tackled her, knocking her out, or so she said. This put paid to my chances, which were probably not as great as I had been led to believe.

***

After the Northern Irish half of our summer, the French half has begun. Nicolas is at ease, and I am now the bewildered one. As soon as we step onto French soil Nicolas is in charge, leading me everywhere, always ahead, always saying 'Come on, Willie'– the one English phrase he allows himself and delights in saying.

He speaks to me in a language that has little in common with anything I have learnt at school, or from Kathleen Davey. This is *argot* – French slang. The police are not *gendarmes* but *flics*. Girls are *nanas* and guys are *mecs*. People you dislike are *salauds* or *cons*. People you like are *sympa*. We smoke cigarettes – *clopes* – Gauloises without filters, nonchalantly opening the blue packet by removing the silver paper over one corner. 'Very' is *vachement* and is very overused.

From Orly we take a bus to the Gare du Nord and a night train to the Midi – the South of France. We sleep on the upper and middle bunks of green couchettes, waking early next morning in Toulouse, where we take a smaller red train to Castres, the administrative centre of the Tarn department.

It is hotter than I've ever known. High summer. This is a different climate. Dappled plane trees line the streets of the small town. Little old men in berets play *pétanque* and drink *pastis*. Nicolas' father picks us up at the station. He is dressed in a jacket and knitted blue tie, not a clerical collar like Dad, and is quiet and austere. I smell the heat, the burning of rubber and melting of asphalt, as the Citroën Dyane, with the steering wheel on the wrong side, winds its way up a hairpin-bended road, through the valley.

We arrive in the tiny village of Saint Salvy de la Balme,

where Nicolas' grandparents own an ancient stone house that backs onto the main street. I am tired and confused and am shown to a bedroom to rest. Someone closes bottle-green shutters and I sleep for I don't know how long. When I awake I wander into a kitchen where Nicolas' mother speaks to me kindly, but I am unable to answer. Everyone is saying 'Ça *va*?' to me and I don't know how to respond. This goes? This goes where? Nicolas, exasperated, explains that the answer to 'Ça *va*?' is '*Oui,* ça *va*'.

It's all very odd. At school I learned how to reply to '*Comment allez-vous*?' or even '*Comment vous portez-vous*?' But I begin to get the hang of it.

Breakfast is warm chocolate in a bowl with no handles. You are supposed to pick it up with both hands. No cereal and no toast. You have to break off part of a stick of bread – a *baguette* – and slice it sideways with a knife.

Nicolas continues to instruct me in the new French language that I must learn. The first evening, as we come down to dinner, he tells me that in France it is customary to thank the person who has cooked the meal and to compliment them on the quality of the food. He tells me that the correct way to say this is '*Putain de Dieu, c'est dégueulasse*'.

I don't know what some of these words mean, but I try to memorise the phrase. At the end of a delicious meal, cooked by his mother, Nicolas nods to me, but I'm afraid I will get the pronunciation wrong. The moment passes. Back in my room I find a French Dictionary and look up the words Nicolas has instructed me to address to his mother: 'God's whore, this food is like vomit'. What a chancer Nicolas is – *Quel salaud!*

***

Over the next ten days I follow Nicolas around St Salvy and neighbouring villages, one step behind, one minute late. I sit on a little motorised bike – a Solex – following his racing bike. When we travel to Lyon he lends me a small urban bike to follow him, and I am often left stranded on the wrong side of several lanes of traffic driving on the right. We stop in a café in the old part of the city where the silk industry was once based. We order an Orangina and smoke our Gauloises cigarettes. Nicolas points out a lady with heavy make-up, sitting in the corner smiling at us. '*C'est une pute – une putain*,' he whispers. I didn't realise that women of this profession existed outside of James Bond books.

Back in Nicolas' house we sit in his room with his friends. They talk politics. We listen to LP records of Bob Dylan – *Blonde on Blonde* – and Leonard Cohen, whose name I first learn in French (*Lé-on—ar Co-en*), and Hugues Aufray, who has translated Dylan into French. I write out the words of 'The day when the ship comes in': '*Le jour où le bateau viendra*', on the squared paper of a notebook. Nicolas is withdrawn. A close friend of his, who was driving a car along a poplar-lined road, fell asleep at the wheel and was injured in an accident, losing part of his leg. I don't have the right words to sympathise.

We hitchhike across the department of la Drôme, and camp in a field. I lie awake all night in our little tent, disturbed by a scratching sound by my head. In the morning there is a hole where the tent has been eaten away and a half-chewed baguette. 'Just a mouse,' says Nicolas, unimpressed by my sensitivity.

A party is being held in an old chateau, by the parents of friends from the church. I am drawn to a beautiful girl, who wears a revealing brown bikini when she swims in the river. She is a clergyman's daughter, called Hélène, but I am incapable of approaching her. In the evening we sit round a fire. We eat a roasted sheep – a *méchoui* – and the wine flows. I am singing '*Chevaliers de la Table Ronde*' and speaking the most fluent French, full of newly acquired slang, to a nineteen-year-old girl who is friendly and finds me cute – *mignon*. I fall asleep and learn later that I have been sick. Some parents have been shocked by my behaviour. French children are gradually introduced to wine, whereas my family are teetotallers, and I've just had a total alcohol immersion course.

Nicolas and his *copains* do not believe in God and do not go to church. I think that must be hard for his father. He is a quiet, thoughtful man, interested in Northern Ireland. He has read Bernadette Devlin's book, *The Price of My Soul*. Back in Lyon we watch the black and white TV and see the Royal Ulster Constabulary baton-charging a crowd in Derry. Nicolas' father asks me why the police are doing this. I try to explain that Ulster is British, because the majority is British, and we want to keep it that way. Civil rights are fine, but the violence is wrong. The pictures are disturbing. The police seem to be more violent than the crowd. Why is that? I feel under attack. Isn't Nicolas' father a Protestant too? Perhaps he looks at it differently, since Protestants are a minority in France. I don't have the answers. What is going on in my country?

***

Pictures of those three weeks in France remain in my mind
fifty years later. In one of them Nicolas' grandfather listens
to me playing a Bach prelude on his piano and shows me his
collection of the works of Sir Walter Scott, first published
in French. In another image I am sitting in the garden in
Saint Salvy, on a large granite boulder, with moss growing
on it. I'm smoking a Gauloise and listening to the crickets
singing. It's after lunch and I've been waiting all day. A
postman arrives, walks across the green grass, and hands
me a folded blue telegram. Written inside, in bad English,
are my O level results, some pleasing, some disappointing.
I have done best in Latin and Greek, the two subjects I
have decided to abandon.

My last memory of Nicolas is on our final day in
Lyon when he has decided that my education in slang is
complete, and that I now need to study classical French.
He takes me to a bookshop and buys me two paperbacks
– *Livres de Poche* – classic novels of 19th-century realism:
Germinal by Émile Zola and *Le Père Goriot* by Honoré de
Balzac. I will go on to study them both at university.

***

In 2000, on the way back to Belgium from a holiday in
Spain, I stopped with my family at Saint Salvy de la Balme,
found the house, and saw the boulder where I had first
read my O level results. I rang the bell, but there was no
answer. I wrote a note and left my address. A few weeks
later a friendly reply arrived from Nicolas' father. He had
been having a siesta in the garden when we called and had
not heard the bell. He was now retired and living in the

village. He remembered me and my visit well. There was now peace in Northern Ireland. As for Nicolas, he had become a cardiologist and would certainly write to me. I'm still waiting for the letter.

Come on, Nicolas. *Maintenant je parle français.*

*Bill Hanna and Honor Boyd
announce their engagement,
1950*

*Me, Dad, John and Mum,
Windsor Manse, 1957*

*Rev. and Mrs William Hanna, at their wedding reception,
Cultra, Co. Down, 28th June 1951*

John and me on our 'new' trikes, with Ruth, Windsor Manse, 1959

John (in Inchmarlo blazer) and me watching the 12th July parade,
Lisburn Road, Belfast, 1959

Me, Anne Louise and John,
playing Cowboys and Indians,
Windsor Manse, 1961

John, Anne Louise and me, 1962

The Minister's wife delivers the first bowl at the Ladies Bowling Club, Windsor Presbyterian Church

With Evelien, Haddington, Scotland, July 1963

Geneva, July 1965

Dad on the platform, St Johnston Carnival, 1979

The Sheriff, Davy Crockett and cowgirl Annie, St Johnston Carnival, 1979

Andy

Karol Wojtyla meets Bill Hanna, Dublin, 1979

Windsor Presbyterian Church and Windsor Manse, 2020

The Braeside above Loughgiel, Co. Antrim

The Old Police Barracks in Loughgiel, Co. Antrim. Cahal Daly's family once lived next door

PART FOUR

My Story

1975–1983

Goodbye
Yellow Brick Road

On 1 January 1973, the United Kingdom, Ireland and Denmark joined the European Economic Community. On 17 March I was vice-captain of the RBAI 1st XV in the Ulster Schools' Cup Final. During the year the IRA took its bombing campaign to England, killing and injuring many people. Political talks continued, and, in December, an agreement to share power between Unionist and Nationalist parties was signed at Sunningdale.

All these events were to affect my life, but the one that mattered most to me at the time was reaching the Ulster Schools' Cup Final. It was my second year playing for the 1st XV. It was exhilarating to stand on the turf of Ravenhill, the rugby ground that until the 1950s had hosted international matches. The final of the Schools' Cup is played there each year on St Patrick's Day. In 1973 17,000 spectators watched and the game was shown on Ulster TV. We were favourites to win, after beating Dad's school, Ballymena Academy, in the semi-final. In the event our team scored twice, once a cheeky effort by scrum-half and captain Colin Patterson, who went on to play for Ireland and the British and Irish Lions, and the second a glorious solo break by the fastest man on our team, Alan McGovern, whose nickname was Haggis, because he was from Scotland. Sadly we lost the kicking encounter and the match, by the score of 13-8, to Ballyclare, a school whose team had never before reached the final.

It's hard to remember much about the game. I was aware of being watched, and trying to impress the spectators, particularly Dad, who was somewhere in the stands. Everything was rapid, faster than any game I had played in before. One of our wingers broke his collarbone in a late rush for the line. The game was over so soon that I could not believe it when the referee blew his final whistle. Pumped up with adrenalin, I wanted to stay on the pitch and play the match all over again. How could it be over already, and how could we have lost? One of my pals cried bitter tears in the changing room. I could not speak.

That summer, as I waited for my A level results, I worked at Butlin's holiday camp in Ayr. The campers were mainly from Glasgow. There were redcoats to entertain them, and Bluebell chorus girls to titillate them. Five enormous pubs were open from morning to night. There were as many security people as entertainers so as to prevent folk from fighting one another after they had 'had a few'. The riskiest time was the weekend of the Glasgow Fair, when the hard men descended on the Scottish holiday camp.

My first job was at the Bingo Bar, washing glasses all

day. Bingo was punctuated by wrestling, impressive to watch on the first day, but predictable by the end of the week, when the choreography of falls became familiar.

A wee lassie from Lanarkshire was my first Catholic girlfriend. She told me that Ulster Protestants were in the minority. I argued with her, as I'd always considered us the majority in Northern Ireland. But she said that since the majority in the island of Ireland was Catholic, the whole country should follow their wishes and join in a United Ireland. This stung me, even though I had to admit to myself that she had a point.

My A level results arrived, not as brilliant as they should have been, but good enough to get me into Edinburgh University, to study French with Contemporary European Institutions. I thought that these studies might one day lead to some kind of job.

The first term at university went by quickly. I had a room in the Pollock Halls of Residence, with other 'overseas' students. Once I was selected for the freshers' rugby team I made many pals, some of whom, like me, also attended law lectures at the Old College.

Only a few boys studied French, perhaps ten out of the 200 students at each lecture. I found myself sitting, for the first time in my educational life, in a room filled with girls: interesting, but also intimidating. At my first tutorial the lecturer decided to take the roll call in French. One after the other ten girls declared themselves '*présente*' (feminine). When my turn came, I was so confused that I blurted out, as my first word in French, '*présente*' (feminine), when I should have declared myself as '*présent*' (masculine). I still blush to think of it.

During the week, after lunch in the Old Students' Union, I would drink half pints of beer, costing 9p each, smoke the pipe Dad had given me to wean me off cigarettes, and listen to jazz music in the basement. The middle-aged saxophonist advised us not to miss a musician making his last tour of the UK. That's how I heard Duke Ellington, one of the greatest jazz pianists and composers of the 20th century, standing on his last legs to conduct his orchestra.

On a Friday evening, early in the New Year of 1974, I went to a play at the King's Theatre, with a girl who had first chatted me up after a history tutorial, and had asked to watch me playing rugby. At the interval she announced that she had a boyfriend who was a sailor. He had returned from sea, and she could no longer see me.

Next day, we lost a scrappy rugby match on a muddy pitch. In the evening I was downing pints in the students' bar at Pollock Halls, bruised by the rugby, and annoyed at being dumped, when a teammate suggested we go to a dance at Ewing Hall.

The event was held in a square room on the ground floor. I lingered at the edge, in a corner of the room, playing angrily with the table football machine, 'nursing my wrath to keep it warm'. I had been dumped, and by someone who had done all the running! Hmmpfh.

Just then a girl came up and asked me to dance. She was wearing a mauve long-sleeved T-shirt, and tight-fitting beige trousers. Her hair was long and chestnut-coloured, with blond streaks bracketing an impossibly sun-tanned face. It was 19 January, but she was wearing no shoes. She looked up at me, appealing, smiling. How could I resist?

Her name was Paola. She was Italian, and had just come

back from spending Christmas in Tanzania where she lived. I found this doubly exotic, and managed to impress her by knowing that Dar es Salaam was her country's commercial capital.

A voice on the dance floor beside us called out, 'I've dropped my contact lens'. Paola left me standing in the middle of the dance floor, and went straight to the doorway, where she turned on all the lights. While the room full of heaving couples groaned in frustration, she scrabbled around the floor, found the lens, and returned it to its owner.

The slow dance was Elton John's 'Goodbye Yellow Brick Road'. After it ended I carried Paola across to my own hall, and all the way up the stairs to my fifth-floor room. She was light and I was fit. I read to her from Robert Louis Stevenson's *Edinburgh*, and gave her an apple. I didn't kiss her yet, but took her back safely, still bare-footed, to her friend's hall where she was staying the night. Paola was studying French and Italian, so I would be able to see her again at my French lectures.

On the following Monday afternoon, as students milled around outside the French lecture theatre, under the David Hume tower, Paola saw me, jumped off the table on which she was sitting, and leapt into my arms, wrapping her legs tightly round me. The whole of Edinburgh was shocked. Onlookers, who happened to include my so recent girlfriend and her group of friends, were dumbfounded. I was delighted, in more ways than one. That was it. We were, and still are today, a couple: *'présente'*, and *'présent'*.

Ulster Strikes Again

The year 1974 was one of promise for me, as it was for the UK and Ireland, as new EEC members. But for Northern Ireland it was another bad year. Decent Protestants and Catholics, looking to a brighter future, had agreed on a power-sharing agreement, but Protestant extremists could not accept the compromise. Within months, paramilitary groups, the Ulster Worker Council, and Paisley's supporters had brought down the new Northern Ireland government. Their action put back the peace process for another twenty years.

In my last year at school I'd learnt how moderate people could be intimidated. When loyalists called a strike, most people stayed away from work, not because they supported the action, but out of fear. No buses ran, as they were often attacked. That wasn't a problem for us, as we walked to school. One day only a few pupils turned up at Inst. It was strange to sit in a class of two or three boys, instead of twenty-six. It was like the time of the Big Freeze in 1963, when so few of us risked going to school, only now our fear was not of being caught in a snowdrift, but of being beaten up by a bunch of thugs.

One of my friends, who had always previously acted the 'hard man', asked to walk home with John and me, seeking the safety of numbers. When we reached the manse, only halfway home for him, he asked if he could borrow some ordinary clothes. He was afraid of appearing in his housing estate wearing the Inst uniform. I learnt that he came from a mixed background. His mother was Catholic, but the family lived in a Protestant estate, and he had to keep a low profile. I lent him a blue jumper and a pair of red trousers, loyalist colours that helped him to reach home unmolested. He later joined the police force.

I was at university when the UWC called their largest strike, including workers at the main power plant near Larne. They were able to bring the province to a standstill. Mum, who had survived Belfast during the Blitz, was not perturbed. She insisted on driving to her work as a nurse tutor, crossing picket lines manned by masked men wielding sticks. Her colleagues and friends in the health service, many of whom were Catholics, felt intimidated and stayed at home. Stormont fell, the power-sharing executive collapsed, and the British Government reimposed direct rule from Westminster.

In response the IRA continued its murderous campaigns. For the next twenty years, Protestant paramilitaries answered tit for tat. My father never saw peace return to Northern Ireland. I became convinced that peace was impossible. People had become too extreme. I decided that there was no future for me in Northern Ireland, and that my destiny lay elsewhere.

L'Été Indien

When Kathleen Davey gave me private French lessons, her eldest son Robbie was spending his third university year as an English language assistant at a school in Bayonne in south-west France. He also played rugby for the Bayonne 1st XV. He became my role model. A few years later, in 1975, I had the same opportunity of spending the third year of my university studies in France. This was a rare privilege, in the days before the EU's Erasmus Programme, which has given millions of European students the chance to study abroad.

Paola also spent the year in France. Because she studied Italian as well as French she was given a cushy posting in a *lycée* in Saint-Raphaël on the Côte d'Azur, not far from the Italian border. As for me, I was sent to a secondary school in Limoges, a city in the middle of France where my law professor, JDB Mitchell, knew one of the university lecturers. The French verb *'limoger'* – 'to send to Limoges' – means to be sent to the back of beyond.

The first days of my *'limogeage'* were lonely, like my first days in Edinburgh, but that changed as soon I found a rugby team. The president of the Irish Rugby Football Union, Harry McKibbin, had obtained an official licence for me to play rugby in France. The nephew of the concierge at my school introduced me to his team, Club Sportif Saviem. When I walked into the changing room for the first time, and was introduced as the new Irish 'rugbyman', one by one each player shook my hand.

At our preparatory course for new language assistants, held in Poitiers, we were advised to be careful how we addressed the French as 'you'. There is a subtle distinction, which does not exist in English, between the formal *'vous'* and the friendly *'tu'*. They told us that it was wise always to start with *'vous'* and only to use *'tu'* after being invited to do so. This was a big mistake with my new French rugby pals. After I had said *'vous'* a couple of times one of them turned to me and said, 'The next time you say *"vous"* to me I will thump you. It's *"tu"* for your teammates, and *"tu"* for the opposition. Even the bloody referee is *"tu"*. Got it?'

Saviem was a branch of the Renault company. They manufactured buses, trucks and tank engines. They joked that after the 1973 Arab-Israeli conflict, the tanks they had sold to the Arabs were returned for repairs by the Israelis. The forwards were tough factory-floor workers, including Coco, a prop with a broken nose, whose preferred sport was boxing. The backs, on the other hand, were managers – superior and temperamental. At training, if the ball wasn't passed correctly from the forwards to our winger, he would throw a tantrum, walk off the pitch and refuse to take any more part in the session. *Voilà!*

After such outbursts forwards and backs usually made up again by going out for a slap-up meal at a top Limoges restaurant. All the good work of training was undone by '*un petit Ricard*', a small pastis, followed by several more, and a three-course meal, well '*arrosé*' with a bottle of Cahors wine. We sang French and Irish songs at table: '*Chevaliers de la Table Ronde*' followed by 'The Wild Rover'.

In Limoges I learnt the best of French rugby and the worst. A French rugby team can be brilliant on its day, but if the opposition begins to niggle at them and get under their skins, they can be awful. Our Saviem team more or less collapsed during the year. At the outset there was a dispute about the trainer, called Expert, who wasn't one. Things improved following his departure, and we had some good matches. However, the team insisted on having a full lunch before an early afternoon kick-off, not the wisest of preparations. Our worst defeat came one winter's day on a muddy pitch at a provincial town called La Souterraine. I still have the report from *Le Populaire*, which informed its readers that the referee had to stop the match in the forty-fifth minute, after some '*very bad gestures*' by our team, '*which included hitting the referee, on several occasions*'.

Why was the poor man treated so? It was simply because the opposition was too good. They scored four tries in a row, and the pugilistic Coco, still under the influence of lunchtime alcohol, expressed his frustration as best he knew, by punching the referee.

It was a sad ending to the season. However, I have good memories of the pals I made on the rugby fields of the Limousin region. Among my souvenirs are a Limoges porcelain breakfast set, gifted to me when I left, and the ability to swear fluently in French – always using the informal '*tu*'.

During the week, when not playing rugby or attending lectures at the university, I taught English at the Guy de Maupassant secondary school. The headmaster lived on the top floor of a house on the school campus. I had a room on the ground floor. He kept a pet crocodile, about six feet long, in his bath. One week, when I had caught flu and had a raging fever, I hallucinated that the reptile had climbed out of its narrow enclosure and was descending the staircase to enter my room.

When I first arrived at the school, the headmaster interviewed me and asked me my nationality.

'*Britannique*.'

'What's that? Are you English?'

'No.'

'Are you Irish, then?'

'Yes.'

'Irish. Good. When he resigned, General De Gaulle visited Ireland. Irish whiskey, *hein*. Irish fighting spirit, *bon*. Rugby, excellent.'

I decided after this to keep things simple and just say I was Irish. Some pupils did not know about Ireland. I had to show on a map that Ireland and Iceland were different places. Others had heard a little about the Troubles. To tell them more, I stencilled copies of 'The Town I Loved So Well', Phil Coulter's ballad about Derry.

Older French people had a romantic view of Ireland. How often did I hear them say that they had never been there, but would love to visit. They had glimpsed our green scenery in the film *Ryan's Daughter*. Teachers proudly showed me their copies of Michel Déon's *The Purple Taxi*, a popular novel set in Ireland. They admired the island to the west that was English-speaking, but not England – the one that was republican and revolutionary, not a monarchy and a rival power. Michel Sardou later sang 'Connemara', a chart-topping ballad that captured the flavour of this island of the French imagination.

In those days, long before computers and mobile phones, when you spent a year abroad, you really were somewhere else. My complete immersion in another culture was only interrupted by Dad's weekly letters with the latest news from home. Although I visited Paola in Saint-Raphaël as often as possible, when I was in Limoges I focussed on mastering all things French. I bought a *mobylette* and learnt how to drive around city streets, taking priority from the right. I ordered a *café crème* at the local café and smoked Gauloises on the *terrasse*, while reading *Le Populaire* and *Le Monde*. There was no TV in my room, but each evening I listened to Jacques Chancel's *Radioscopie* on the radio. We went to the cinema each week to see the most recent French films, starring Catherine Deneuve, Alain Delon and Jean-Paul Belmondo. We listened to and learnt all the latest '*chansons*'. I arrived in September to Joe Dassin's '*L'Été Indien*' and consoled myself with his ballad '*Ça va pas changer le monde*'. I read the novels by Zola and Balzac that Nicolas had given me in 1971, and also devoured what the French really read – San Antonio – humorous police novels, written in idiosyncratic slang. I bought LPs by Serge Lama and Jacques Brel, and listened to Aragon's poems, sung by Jean Ferrat.

Alain Texier, Professor Mitchell's friend in the Limoges University Law Faculty, helped me to prepare my 10,000-word *mémoire* in French. We chose the topical subject of French Regionalisation. He and his wife invited me to their home and taught how the French structure their thought and language. I will always be grateful to them for their kindness and tutoring. I hadn't learnt much French in Edinburgh, and almost failed my second year. Living in France for one year taught me more about its people and language than I would have learnt in a lifetime of French studies in Scotland.

In July I joined Paola in Saint-Raphaël. It was the year of the Montreal Olympics, one of the hottest summers on record. We stayed with one of her teacher friends, occupying a tent at the bottom of her garden. One night, after a downpour, I found my copy of Proust's *A l'ombre des jeunes filles en fleurs* floating at the bottom of the tent. I dried it out on a rock, unstuck the pages and read the thick volume twice.

Paola found me a job in a café, but I couldn't get the hang of the coffee machine, and was sacked after the first day. I made a better job of selling doughnuts on the topless beaches of the Côte d'Azur. With my summer earnings I bought a small typewriter on which Paola's mother typed out the final version of my *mémoire*. The result persuaded Prof Mitchell that my *limogeage* had been worthwhile. It made the difference between an average degree and a good one and put me on the road to the College of Europe in Bruges, Belgium.

What a Difference
a D Makes

Dad was plain William Hanna, and to his friends, Bill. To distinguish between us he gave me the middle name David, after one of his mentors, the Scottish evangelist DP Thompson.

In 1975, after twenty-five years as minister in Belfast, Dad accepted a call from the congregations of St Johnston and Ballylennon, in County Donegal. That summer we left Belfast and journeyed seventy miles west to the small village of St Johnston, just a few miles across the border. Our new home was a handsome manse that looked over the wide and bending River Foyle from the Republic towards Northern Ireland.

Dad was rejuvenated by leaving the city and returning to the countryside. He had been a student in Derry, a few miles down the river, and he knew the area well. He became friendly with the parish priest and set up a Village Improvement Committee, with the aim of enhancing the look of the rundown village and encouraging good relations between Catholic and Protestant neighbours. Dad revelled in the familiarity of village life and the novelty of residing in the Republic of Ireland. Mum was happy as well, commuting to her nursing management job in Magee College, Derry. One of her good colleagues there was Paddy Hume, a brother of John Hume, who later won the Nobel Peace Prize.

It was a joyful time for Mum and Dad, an Indian summer. The villagers were friendly. When we wound up the ancient telephone and asked the local operator to connect us to a neighbour, she would often know whether the person was in or out. On Saturdays we strolled down to the cricket pitch by the river and watched the village team play in the North-West League. We were on first-name terms with the young Gardaí – the national police.

The following Easter I returned from my year in France for a couple of weeks. One day I drove the family car through the towns of Ballybofey and Stranorlar. Soon after returning to France and getting stuck into my *mémoire*, I received one of Dad's weekly letters, typed on airmail paper.

Friday evening 9.p.m.
9th April 1976

and Hello to you this Spring-like day.
This afternoon at 1 pm as the two blue uniformed Gardaí came up the drive and swung into the back yard I gave them my usual cheery greeting and said: 'Now gentlemen there

you are. I have you just where I want you. All I have to do is close that gate behind you and you are at my mercy'.

'Aha,' said Declan, as he switched off his engine in the great big Ford marked GARDA. 'Aha indeed, Reverence, but I am afraid the boot is on the other foot. I am sorry to inform you that you were found speeding at 48 mph on the Stranorlar Road the week before last, and here is the official communication from the Commission for Prosecutions.'

To which I replied, 'Interesting you should bring up this affair, Declan. I have been aware that Mrs Lapsley was feeding you fellows too many rich starchy spuds and I now see it is detrimental to the eyesight. For one thing Declan, me boy — this old bus against which I am leaning is not capable of 48 mph, especially on the sort of trashy fuel that I buy down the drive from your man, but also if you lift those baby-blue eyes of yours again to the aforementioned document, you will discover to your amazement that the name of your culprit is William D. Hanna, not that a D makes a D... of difference to the gravamen of your accusation. However, I am happy to inform you that the above-named has fled the country — absconded — cleared out, buzzed, done a bunk, as they say, and, to put it delicately, you are barking up a lamp-standard with no bulb at the end of it. In other words, as Old Man Dev used to say with his Spanish accent, "céad mile failte".'

To which the gallant Declan replied with a deep sigh of relief, 'So the felon is no longer in the jurisdiction?' 'That was the general thread of my statement' I answered soberly. Thereupon Declan politely offered me a cigarette, which I refused... Never allow yourself to be bought by the opposition has always been my position. As the two gendarmes swung into reverse on the concrete back yard, we waved each other the cheeriest of goodbyes, and muttering the ancient maxim to the effect 'There but for the grace of God', I went indoors and fixed myself some lunch, which I found surprisingly tasty.

After much cogitation on the above I am convinced that if you get a short back and sides and remove all fungus from your face you might with luck slip into the country on an unapproved road (so long as you wear a hat and gloves) and the bright Declan will be none the wiser.

Sorry, Lad, for as your Mum has remarked, I've played that fish enough. What actually did happen was that Declan with much relief tore up the summons and we spent the next twenty minutes discussing John Hume and Garret FitzGerald who spoke at the big conference the previous evening.

We are full of hope that John will be home by the weekend. Andy is now on holidays. Do hope that old essay of yours is now air-borne. Best of luck. Keep in touch. Dad

The Road to Dublin

In 1977, during my final term at Edinburgh University, I had an interview with the British Council in London for a scholarship to study European law at the College of Europe in Bruges. Just when it seemed that the interview was over, one of the panel had a final question. She remarked on my address in Donegal, and asked me, 'You are British, aren't you?' 'Of course,' I replied, without hesitation.

This question struck me as unfair. I had been brought up as British and had a UK passport. But I also felt entirely at ease being Irish. So what if my parents recently moved from Belfast to Donegal? How could that alter who I was or make me more or less acceptable to the British Council?

My answer must have reassured them, for they awarded me the scholarship. To this day I am grateful. In the charming old Flemish city of Bruges I was one of 130 students who came from all over Europe to study European integration through two languages: French and English.

At the beginning of our year we tended to form national groups, each of which was expected to organise a party. There were a few English students, but I fitted in more easily with the Irish. On St Patrick's Day we hosted our national party. We obtained sponsorship from the Irish Representation in Brussels, which allowed us to offer everyone Guinness and Irish coffee. I led the singing of 'The Wild Rover', with Joe from Limerick, Finn from Norway and Ferdinand from Austria.

Paola and I were engaged to be married and we needed to find jobs. I was eager to join the European Commission, but five years' work experience was required before you could take part in a competition. Joining a national diplomatic service was one way of gaining relevant experience, but which should I choose? The UK Foreign Office, or the Irish Department of Foreign Affairs?

Hedging my bets, I applied for both, but when I was called to London and Dublin on the same day, I had to make a choice. Spurred on by my Irish friends I wrote to a previous Irish student, who had gone on from the College to join the Department of Foreign Affairs. He sent me an encouraging reply. Other soundings with Northern Irish friends convinced me that Ireland favoured the European project more than Britain, and was likely to value my studies more highly. So I chose Dublin, a decision I never regretted, not least when, forty years later, Britain decided to leave the EU.

Back in 1978, in a gap between tough competition law exams, I flew via Paris to Dublin. Anne Louise came down from Donegal to meet me, bringing with her my one good suit. In the morning I had a short haircut on Grafton Street, and coffee with Andy in Bewleys. In the afternoon my interview was chaired by a friendly and disarming assistant secretary.

None of the panel asked me about myself or my motivation. No one enquired, 'You are Irish, aren't you?' The entire interview was a general knowledge test. I floundered on many questions, even one about the Plantation of Ulster. Which counties of Ulster were planted? Most people will think of Antrim and Down, but these counties were not, in fact, part of the official 17th-century Plantation.

Had the selection panel realised how little I knew about Irish politics and government they would perhaps have thrown me out of the interview to go busking on Grafton Street. I didn't even know the name of the Minister for Foreign Affairs. But my overnight reading of an Irish history book helped with one or two answers. I knew the names of the United Irish leaders of 1798, which seemed to please the panel, as did my accent in French. Most importantly I was benefitting from Garret FitzGerald's decision, when he was Minister for Foreign Affairs, to open the department to Northern Protestants, by removing the obligation to know the Irish language and allowing equal credit for another language – in my case French. I left the interview sure that I had failed, but pleased that I had kept my cool under fire. Perhaps the questions were less designed to test what I knew, than to see how I would respond when I was out of my depth.

A couple of months later, to my surprise and delight, an official letter arrived in St Johnston Manse calling me for a medical examination in Dublin, subject to which I was to be offered the job of Third Secretary in the Department of Foreign Affairs.

Iona

———

Paola and I were married on 22 July 1978 at St Columba's Church, Upanga, Dar es Salaam.

My whole family – Mum, Dad, John and Anne Louise – travelled with me to Tanzania for the wedding. Paola's sister Silvia and brother-in-law Gino were there too. The reception was held in Paola's parents' garden, in Kinondoni Road.

The church ceremony was performed by the local church of Scotland minister, assisted by Dad, who gave an address, and Padre Carlo, a priest who said a prayer in Italian, despite Paola's refusal to promise to him that she would bring up our children as Catholics. The congregation was mostly made up of Italians, unfamiliar with the Presbyterian hymns and ceremony.

Anne Louise was a bridesmaid and Paola's niece Diana and nephew Diego were also dressed up for the occasion.

Diego was only a few years old and had been given a Mickey Mouse watch to wear. At the most solemn moment in the ceremony he realised that he had forgotten it and called out, '*Ci siamo dimenticati gli orologi!*' – 'We've forgotten the watches!'

In his address Dad talked about St Columba, also known as Colmcille, after whom the church was named. He was an abbot and prince in the 6th century who established monasteries all over Ireland. His greatest foundation was at Iona, in the western isles of Scotland. From there the gospel was brought to Scotland and on to England. Iona became the leading centre of Christian learning in north-west Europe. The monks wrote and decorated illuminated gospels, the most famous of which is the Book of Kells, sent for safety to Ireland when the Vikings began their attacks on the monasteries at the beginning of the 8th century.

Dad said, '*We meet today in St Columba's Church. You have heard me talk in the past about Columba, that wild Irishman who succeeded in bringing the gospel to Scotland. When Columba met the Western Islanders of Scotland he said to them, "Let me tell you about God's will for you. His will is better farming, better fishing and better souls." Let me attempt to translate that into language for this day. The will of God for you both is a happy home and a fulfilling career, with the spirit of God as a protecting roof over your heads. A blessed Trinity, cultivate all three and the blessing of the Highest will be yours. God richly bless you both.*'

When he talked of the roof protecting us, Dad had in mind the abbey in Iona. George MacLeod, the radical preacher he listened to on the radio in the 1930s, had established a new community there. He brought together young clergymen like Dad and unemployed workers from the slums of Glasgow to rebuild the abbey. Dad spent one summer working on the roof.

Paola and I visited Iona a few years ago. It's a small island off Mull. The abbey is simple and built in beautiful stone. There is a yellow sand beach, where the monks were slaughtered in AD 806 by the Vikings, and in the sands nestles a nine-hole golf course. Iona is where Ireland and Scotland meet. It's a place of learning, where the power of the Word overcame the darkness. I felt there the presence of my father and of generations past. When the time comes, I'd like my ashes to be spread on the beach on Iona.

The Third Secretary

Three weeks after our wedding in Dar es Salaam, Paola and I landed at Dublin airport, bronzed and beaming from our honeymoon spent in the Manyara and Ngorongoro parks of Northern Tanzania. She was twenty-four years of age, and I was twenty-three. We felt that we were playing a game of being grown-ups. We rented an upstairs flat in Goatstown, in South Dublin. I was starting a new life in a new city, with a job that paid a salary, and the prospect of a career seeing the world. Paola found freelance translating and interpreting work for the Industrial Development Agency and the Export Board – Córas Tráchtála – that took her all over the country.

On 14 August 1978 I alighted from the 62 bus, wearing a new green three-piece suit, bought at C&A. I crossed St Stephen's Green and entered the portals of Iveagh House. It was the height of the summer break, and many civil servants were on holiday – their 'holliers' as the posher South Dubliners called them. On my first day as an Irish civil servant I met an official from the personnel department. This kind gentleman, rumoured to have never travelled outside the country, had a standard pep talk about two great perils of the diplomatic life: the temptations of drink and of women. However, since the other third secretary joining the department that day was a young woman, we were only warned about the evils of drink. Next we were asked for our names in Irish. I had no idea what mine was. But it was important to record this information, because one day, in the fullness of time, we would become ambassadors, and our names would have to be written in Irish on the letters of accreditation.

Although I was embarrassed not to know Irish, I was thrilled by the prospect of one day becoming an ambassador. At lunchtime I found a bookshop and ascertained that my Irish name was Liam Ó hAnnaidh. I wrote this out carefully on a piece of paper. In the afternoon I handed over my Irish credentials to the official, who seemed satisfied with my first day's work.

The next day I was assigned to the Economics Section, which occupied a Georgian house at 52 St Stephen's Green. I was shown to a desk between my boss, the first secretary, who enjoyed the window view of the garden, and the clerical assistant who sat in front of filing cabinets. At lunchtime a fine fellow with a pencil moustache arrived and told me that I was sitting in his chair. That was how my predecessor learned, to his chagrin, that he had been reassigned to the Protocol Section.

A few days later I was called in to meet the Assistant

Secretary for Economic Affairs. A large soft-handed man with ginger hair, he inhabited a spacious front room looking over the Green. Sitting behind an impressive mahogany desk he enquired, in a high-pitched voice, if I knew how to write speeches. The only speeches I had ever written were as best man at two weddings. The assistant secretary seemed disappointed with this and dismissed me. Today I expect third secretaries are trained in how to write speeches. But there was no organised training for us at that time. We learnt everything on the job.

My assignment was to the Energy, Science and Technology desk – subjects for which I had no qualifications whatsoever. This did not seem to matter. My first secretary and immediate boss was an Oxford graduate. My work mainly consisted of drafting notes – with pen and paper – to other government departments. These started with the Irish opening 'A Chara' – 'O Friend' – followed by 'I am directed by the Minister for Foreign Affairs to ...' and asked for views on various EC proposed directives in the field of energy, ending with 'Mise le meas' – 'It is I, with respect'. My boss corrected the English part of my drafts and placed them in his out tray for the clerical assistant, a red-haired young girl from Donegal, whose job was to take them to be typed up by 'the girls' in the typing pool.

My boss wore thick glasses and often seemed to have his head in the clouds. He also showed great interest in my Northern Irish background. He took to inviting me to lunch at the Berni Inn, opposite the side entrance to Trinity College, where he quizzed me on everything I knew about 'the North'. Like many of his colleagues, he had never been there. He was clever and ambitious and soon left the department to become adviser to the Taoiseach, later playing a key role in the peace process.

Dublin was a quiet and relaxed city at that time. Many civil servants were gifted amateurs, language graduates and poets and writers in the tradition of Brian O'Nolan, alias Flann O'Brien. They were not expected to arrive at work too early in the morning, and sometimes returned from lunch late in the afternoon. I pity civil servants today, tied to computers and phones, even at home and at the weekends, always at the beck and call of their bosses. Our days were more leisurely. We arrived at the department at about 9.30 and spent the first hour reading the papers, especially *The Irish Times*. At coffee with the other third secretaries, we talked about who had had the good fortune to be posted to an embassy abroad, and how long it would take for our turn to come. The other third secretaries were talented young people, many of whom went on to have brilliant careers in the Irish Foreign Service or in international organisations. It was like a family. Indeed, there were so many brothers and sons, that other civil servants referred to our department as 'Foreign Affairs & Sons'. Although I knew no one to start with, and came from a different background from most, I was happy to be part of this elite group.

After a year in 52, moving from the Energy desk to Transport, I was sent to the Political Section in Iveagh House to work on the Middle East desk. On my first day there I took a phone call from a Jewish woman who complained at length about a speech given by the minister Brian Lenihan, in which he had called for the creation of a Palestinian state.

With no previous knowledge of the Middle East, and no training about the region, I was clueless about the significance of this statement, but it had seriously riled supporters of Israel. On a visit to Bahrain, the minister had apparently made the statement off the cuff, and it had no doubt gone down well with his Arab audience.

A few days later, Brian Lenihan was back in Ireland and his officials were trying to work out how to backtrack on his speech. At the time it was agreed amongst EEC member states to talk of the desirability of a Palestinian 'homeland', but not of a 'state' with the qualities of independence this implied. The minister was due to answer questions in the lower house of the Irish parliament, the Dáil, in a late evening session, and this would give the opportunity to correct the record. However, Brian Lenihan, known for his plain talking and exuberance, flatly refused to follow his officials' advice. Instead of retreating he advanced, repeating his call for the creation of a Palestinian state, ending with the words 'That is our policy'.

What was to be done? In those days a stenographer recorded verbatim the words of speakers in the Dáil. These were typed up and checked before being published and released to the press. Late that evening we looked together at the record. There was no mistaking it. There in black and white were the fatal words 'That is our policy'. The political director was disconsolate. How was he going to explain this repeated faux pas at the next meeting of his European colleagues? He examined the wording carefully, looking for a solution. 'Perhaps we could change the T to a W, and add a question mark: 'What is our policy?'

It was serious, but also fun, like being on the set of an

Irish version of *Yes, Minister*. I was learning on the job how civil servants and their political masters interact. I also soon learnt the risks of dealing with the press. I had overheard that the Taoiseach had travelled to Libya to do some deal with Colonel Gaddafi, perhaps Libyan oil for Irish beef. One morning my phone rang and it was the political editor of *The Irish Times*. He asked if it were true that Charlie Haughey had gone to Libya. I hesitated for a moment, wondering how to reply. That was enough for the editor, who thanked me and put down the phone. The headline in *The Irish Times* the next day was '*Foreign Affairs do not deny that Taoiseach is in Libya*'. I found out the hard way that you can make a headline even by saying nothing. It is always better to have something prepared to say. I was advised afterwards that all telephone press enquiries were to be addressed to the Press Section. Perhaps such advice could have been given to me on day one.

When Charlie Haughey was chosen as Taoiseach I felt uncomfortable. It was alleged that he had been involved in illegal gunrunning in 1969/70, and it was an open secret that he was involved in crooked dealings. Charlie Haughey's corruption was eventually exposed and his career ended in disgrace.

My lack of knowledge of Irish was sometimes a drawback. Our ambassador in the Lebanon phoned one day with a confidential message to pass on about the Irish contingent of UN peacekeepers. He only wanted to speak in Irish. Fortunately I was able to pass him over to my roommate, who pacified him with his first-class-degree Irish. Afterwards I started Irish Linguaphone lessons at Trinity College.

Dublin was an exciting place for me in the late 1970s, even if for other Dubliners it was stifling. It was certainly safer and more hopeful than Belfast. The poor country I had visited in the 1960s was slowly beginning to develop, thanks to EEC subsidies, and the opportunities of the new Common Market. Young people could choose to stay at home rather than emigrating. I bought a book by Patrick Keatinge called *A Place Among the Nations: Issues of Irish Foreign Policy*. Ireland had a new confidence in international affairs, and I was a part of it.

In the second half of 1979 Ireland assumed the presidency of the European Communities. Everyone in the department was involved. I was roped in for protocol duty at the summit held in Dublin Castle. My job was to ensure that as each head of state and government left the meeting, their official car would be called forward in the correct order from the lower car park to whisk them away. However, when the British Prime Minister, Mrs Thatcher, decided to walk out early, in protest over not getting 'my money back', I was unable to prevent the chauffeur of the French president from racing into pole position, placing his Peugeot 604 in front of the British Jaguar. Mrs T was obliged to stand in the lobby, visibly fuming, while the elegant Valery Giscard d'Estaing, the main opponent of any budgetary rebate for the UK, descended the staircase, passed by the prime minister and departed from the castle ahead of her.

On 28 March 1980, at 7.19 pm by the clock in the ward, our daughter Luisa was born at Mount Carmel Hospital. Daffodils, forsythia and cherry blossoms were out. I was twenty-five years old, and this was the happiest day of my life so far, a joy repeated with the births of David in 1982 and Emilia in 1985. When I celebrated with a pint of Guinness at a pub on Leeson Street, the barman asked me if it was 'a boy or a child'. Back at Mount Carmel, Paola also enjoyed bottled Guinness, supposed to encourage the flow of milk.

At the end of the year the same personnel officer who had first welcomed me to the department called four of us into his room and told us we would now be posted abroad. Each of us had all been waiting for this moment since the day we arrived. We were about to be sent to the ends of the earth to represent Ireland.

The official enjoyed his moment of power. He asked the first chap to guess where he was going to be posted. 'Washington,' he said. 'Correct.' Then it came to me. 'Brussels?' 'Correct.'

I tried to hide my disappointment. I had joined up to see the world and would only see Belgium, once more. What if the decisions were being taken on the spot, giving each of us the post we mentioned? What a fool I had been. Oh, why hadn't I answered 'Washington' or 'Buenos Aires'?

In the event my posting to the Permanent Representation of Ireland to the European Communities in Brussels was a perfect career move. It took me to the heart of Europe, where my knowledge of French and of European institutions was an asset. Brussels turned out to be the only foreign posting I had for the Department of Foreign Affairs. After five years working for the Irish government I had acquired enough experience to be eligible to become a European civil servant. An economic crisis was then raging in Ireland, and we were encouraged to find positions in the

European institutions, which needed more Irish nationals. After a successful competition I applied to work in the part of the European Commission – DG VIII – that dealt with relations with developing countries. Over the following thirty-five years I lived and worked in Brussels, and in six different and fascinating capital cities in the Caribbean, Africa, Latin America and Asia. In my next book I'll write about my life and experience of those places.

Solemnly Meeting the Pope

When Dad retired from Donegal in 1981, a young colleague, Reverend John McVeigh, recalled in a farewell speech one of the highlights of his ministry.

> 'On 29 September 1979 two men met and shook hands. One was the humble moderator of the Synod of Dublin, representing the few thousand Presbyterians who reside in the Irish Republic; the other was the Bishop of Rome, spiritual head of millions of Catholics throughout the world. Did Karol Wojtyla, John Paul II, recognise in the firm handshake and alert smile of Bill Hanna a man like himself in energy, determination and faith?'

When John Paul II came to Ireland, it was the first time a pope had visited the country. Nearly three million people turned out to welcome him at five venues: a remarkable number when you consider that the population of the Republic was then 3.3 million. Some folk must have travelled across the country to catch a glimpse of the pontiff in different places.

It is hard today to appreciate the massive impact of this visit. At that time Ireland was a predominantly Catholic country, and most people attended Mass on Sundays. The Catholic Church and its moral teaching held sway over the government. Its influence reached deep into everyone's lives. When Paola and I arrived in Dublin, newly married, we learnt that we were unable to buy contraceptives from a pharmacy; we had to smuggle them in from the North.

At that time Europe was still divided by the 'Iron Curtain', which ran through Germany, with one part in the West and one in the East. The Berlin Wall, physical manifestation of the separation, was still in place. The countries of Central and Eastern Europe were under the tight grip of the communist Soviet Union. The USSR had sent in its tanks to quash rebellions in Hungary in 1956 and in Czechoslovakia in 1968. However, in Poland a new movement called Solidarity had sprung up in the shipyards of Gdansk. Its leader, Lech Wałęsa, sought to bring about new freedoms. And there was great hope when another Pole, Karol Wojtyla, was elected pope. He spoke many languages and was a charismatic leader, in contrast to his predecessor, the reserved Italian Pope Paul VI.

The new pope's visit to Ireland came soon after the IRA had assassinated Lord Mountbatten, Prince Philip's uncle, near his holiday home in Mullaghmore, County Sligo. Tensions were high, and it was decided it would be too dangerous for the Pope to visit Northern Ireland. However, the Catholic Church sent out invitations to all denominations to meet the Pope in Dublin. The moderator of the Presbyterian Church in Ireland turned down his invitation, but an invitation was also sent to the moderator of the Synod of Dublin. That was Dad.

As Dad described in his memoirs, he came from a mixed community in County Antrim, and knew and respected his Catholic neighbours there. He continued to do so in Belfast, in the mixed Derryvolgie Avenue, with Windsor Presbyterian Church at one end and St Bridget's Catholic church at the other. He was proud of his role as member of the board, and chairman for one year, of St Louise's Girls school on the Falls Road. He had great admiration for Sister Genevieve, the principal of St Louise's who made her Catholic school a haven in the heart of one of the most violent areas of the city. He never shirked from attending meetings at St Louise's, even in the evenings, believing that his clerical collar protected him. When the invitation to meet the Pope came to him he had no doubt that it was his Christian duty, as well as an honour, to accept. But even if Dad had no qualms about travelling to Dublin to meet John Paul II, the visit was kept quiet. Had they known in advance, some of the St Johnston Orangemen, whose attitudes could try my father's patience, might have protested. This visit was the Orangemen's worst nightmare – the whole mass of Catholic Ireland welcoming the figure they had been taught to revile.

Even though the encounter was supposed to be hush-

hush, it was widely talked about in a village where few secrets escaped the telephone operator. When Dad returned home to Donegal, the only question on everyone's lips, including the Orangemen, was '*What was he like?*'

The Pope's visit to Ireland was a success, the forerunner of many visits to countries all over the world. John Paul II became an international superstar. The visit was also politically significant in Ireland. In Drogheda the Pope made a powerful plea to the paramilitaries to lay down their arms:

> '*I wish to speak to all men and women engaged in violence… I appeal to you in language of passionate pleading. On my knees, I beg you to turn away from the path of violence and to return to the ways of peace.*'

It was said at the time that this appeal was so heartfelt, and the personality so powerful that some terrorists considered giving up their campaign, for a while at least. It was only recently that I learned the identity of the Irishman who wrote those words for the Pope to deliver.

In the later years of his pontificate Pope John Paul II turned out to be a more divisive figure, conservative and unwilling to embrace change. In the 1980s and 1990s the Catholic Church was rocked by scandals of sexual abuse of children within Church institutions, carried out by Church personnel and covered up by Church authorities. The Church lost much of its moral standing and credibility. As Ireland's economy prospered from its membership of the European Union, and Irishmen and women became richer and freer, many turned their backs on the church. One lasting sequel of the visit, at that time when contraception was not freely available, was the many Irish children born in 1980 who were named John or Paul or John Paul.

A couple of months after the Pope's visit a large yellow envelope with Italian stamps arrived in St Johnston Manse. It was from the Vatican Observer and contained a photo of the moment Karol Wojtyla shook hands with William Hanna. The contrast between the white of the Pope's garments and Dad's Presbyterian black is striking. I wonder what words they exchanged. No doubt my father, in his County Antrim brogue, said something like, 'You are very welcome to Ireland, sir', to which the Pope replied, in his strong Polish accent, 'Thank you. God bless you'.

In Raymond Calvert's wicked ballad, his hero, William Bloat, *'in the face of death, with his latest breath, solemnly cursed the Pope.'* There is a fair dose of Belfast black humour, and a certain respect for the enemy, in William Bloat's attitude. I'm proud that William Hanna 'solemnly met the Pope'.

I'll never know what Dad said to the Pope John Paul, but I do know what Uncle Robin said when he met him the next year. Uncle Robin had been appointed Director of the Irish School of Ecumenics in Dublin, a joint Catholic-Protestant endeavour. He met John Paul II in Rome, as part of an ecumenical visit. When the Pope concluded the interview with Uncle Robin by saying he would pray for him, Uncle Robin replied, 'And I will pray for you too'.

The Wearing of the Green

'Dad, what happened?'

My father's face looked down at me, gradually coming into focus. I was lying on my back on a bench in the changing rooms at Stade Fallon in Brussels. It was a Sunday morning in November 1982. I had been playing rugby for BUC, a team in the Belgian Second Division, and the last thing I remembered was trying to keep my eye focussed on a high ball coming down straight towards me.

'You did your usual thing. You caught the ball and ran forward, straight at the opposition, and right into a short-arm tackle'.

Jean-Pierre Stasser, our scrum-half, confirmed Dad's account a few minutes later, as he and the rest of our team joined me in the changing rooms after the match.

'It was their No 8. *Le salaud*. The dirty bastard. The English ref saw it, but he did nothing. I don't think he likes you.'

Dad was a better rugby player than me. I had a couple of trials for the Ulster Schools team, but he captained a team that won the Ulster Senior Cup. He played a full season for Edinburgh University 1st XV; I managed to make the Edinburgh 1st XV in my second year, when several first-choice wing-forwards were injured. In all I played for the 1st XV six times and scored one try – a charge down at Craiglockhart. One Saturday we stayed on after our own match to watch British Universities play French Universities, and there popped up my school pal Colin Patterson, now scrum-half of the British University team. He was already being talked of as a possible Irish player and I promised him that I would be present on the day he won his first cap for Ireland.

And so it was that in 1977, while I was studying in Belgium, I learnt from one of Dad's letters that Colin had been chosen as reserve to replace Johnny Moloney on the Irish team due to play France in Paris. Alistair McKibbin, who had been a few years younger at school, was already on the Irish team. Another Ulsterman, the elegant Mike Gibson, one of the greatest Irish players of all time, was playing on the wing, at the end of his career.

In those days there were no cheap Ryanair flights, and few Irish spectators were expected to make the trip for an away match in France. Rugby was still an amateur sport, and no replica shirts were on sale for supporters. On the day of the match, when the final tram was announced, the coach handed green jerseys to the chosen fifteen players.

Each member of the Irish team was allotted six tickets for family and friends. Somehow Dad managed to get me one of the tickets. I've kept the brief telegram:

'Meet Colin at Hotel Terminus'

On the morning of the match I took the train from Brussels to Paris, arrived at the Gare du Nord and went by metro to the hotel. I walked through the revolving door, and there in front of me in the lobby was a group of players made up of Mike Gibson, Colin Patterson, and Alistair McKibbin, standing talking with the Irish coach, Noel Murphy. I walked towards them nervously, but Colin immediately recognised me and introduced me to the famous circle. I was right at the heart of the Irish rugby team about to play France.

That day a second-row forward, by the name of Emmet O'Rafferty, was due to get his first cap. He was a big fellow with a full red beard, not unlike my own. However, he had sustained a knee injury in training and it was doubtful if he would play. When I shook hands with Noel Murphy he looked puzzled and said to me, 'How's the knee?'

I didn't know what to answer. I smiled and mumbled something like 'Very pleased to meet you'. But Colin understood. He turned to me and whispered.

'He thought you were O'Rafferty. You should've said "*The knee's all right. Where's the jersey?*" and you would have made the team.'

And what an Irish team it was. The back row was composed of Fergus Slattery and Willie Duggan of Blackrock College and Stewart McKinney of Dungannon. They faced the French *troisième ligne* of Jean-Claude Skrela, Jean-Pierre Bastiat (described by commentator Bill McLaren as 'an Eiffel Tower of a man') and the blond bombshell Jean-Pierre Rives.

As it was, poor Emmet O'Rafferty did not recover in

time from his knee injury and was replaced by Harry Steele of Ballymena. O'Rafferty never played for Ireland. France won the match. Colin didn't replace Moloney that day, but he soon made it onto the team and played eleven times in a row for Ireland, scoring five tries. He partnered Ollie Campbell at half back on a winning tour of Australia and was also chosen for the British Lions tour of South Africa in 1980. He played in three Tests, before his career came to an end at the age of twenty-five, after a knee injury.

As for me, I ended my rugby career in the depths of the Belgian Second Division, still running straight into trouble, as Dad pointed out. But one Saturday, long ago in Paris, I almost wore the green jersey of Ireland.

The Girl from Armoy

Retirement Row
42 Lough Moss Park
Carryduff
Belfast 8

Monday 14th February 1983

To my fellow typists and other pen pushers,
I say, Dear Friends, don't count on this epistle being of the usual dimensions — for I have just encountered a snag in my ribbon spool — for the blessed apparatus gave up with me on Friday evening, just as I was about to commit to posterity the next thrilling and engrossing installment of my Memoirs.
So, may I speak to Willie first? By the time you get this, Sir, you will have been to Dublin and collected

*the little ticket from Paul Kavanagh. And may you see
an epic encounter on the green sward of Lansdowne
Road! By that time Honor and I will be on our way to
Donegal for the next session of preaching — Raphoe
and Ballindrait this time. And a little tale for you. I
went along to Ravenhill on Tuesday afternoon to collect
the ticket. In front of me was a female of about 30 years
collecting her bundle of stand tickets for her club. She
had a provincial accent you could cut with a knife and
she was in a little bit of personal trouble, having just
lost the heel of a shoe. The lady handing our tickets
was trying to be helpful and to indicate where on the
Cregagh Road there was to be found a heel bar. After
waiting patiently for a few minutes I stepped forward
and said, 'You are in trouble I hear, may I take you back
to the top of the Ormeau Road where I happen now
to be going?' As we left the precinct I said to the fair
damsel, 'I see you are keen on the game. Which club
do you represent?' 'Armoy,' said she. 'Good gracious me,'
said the driver. 'Do you tell me that.' When I heard there
was rugby in Armoy I got as big a thrill as I got when
we started the game in Randalstown. We exchanged
names and we found our Heel Bar. Sadly, Willie, she
did not offer to do an exchange of tickets.*

*Paola, do you remember advising me, before
starting to write my life story, to get hold of 'Experiences
of an Irish RM' and to read it first? We have just had
a splendid TV series of five episodes from the book
with a great cast of English and Irish characters. The
subtle deviousness of the Southern Irish character has
never to my mind been better illustrated. The players*

they brought in from the Abbey Theatre just reveled in their parts, and the big handsome innocent Peter Bowles was perfectly cast as the English Major. Best laugh we've had in a long time.

A very pleasant Sunday in Armagh yesterday, taking the service in First Church, possibly the loveliest building in our denomination.

Left Honor off this evening at Aldergrove on her way to London where four of her students are at work. She will meet up with John and Andy while there. And she has just this moment phoned to say 'Safely landed'. Bless her. Better she than me for this kind of life. On my way home to town, I took the high road by Ligoniel for a change. It was well worthwhile, for the roads were deserted and the lofty view over the city lights was as grand as ever. If only we could get back on the Path of Peace again...

John R.B. on Saturday with his team defeated Ballymena IV by 23-0. Both Inst and Ballymena Academy are nicely placed for a possible appearance on St Patrick's Day at Ravenhill. But the team I am most anxious to see there is Rainey Endowed, Magherafelt, if you please. And for a special reason. Last time at Ravenhill they fielded a three-fold side — five Protestants, five Catholics and five Asians.

Finally, a promise. A new ribbon next week. Am sure you can't wait.

David and Luisa, please don't get cross with Mum and Dad — they are only doing their best.

Con amore molto

Dad XXXX 00

Walking with My Father

The last time I saw Dad was in November 1982 when my parents visited us in Brussels. Luisa was two years old and David was just a baby. We lived in the Flemish suburb of St Genesius Rode. One day we went for a walk in the forest of Soignes, the most glorious feature of the Belgian capital. The woods and forest stretch from the elegant Avenue Louise almost to Waterloo. The forest is mainly made of handsome and tall beech trees. That day they were arrayed in their autumn beauty. Some leaves had fallen to the forest floor, while others remained on the fine branches, yellow and gold, brown and copper. More would fall in December, but some would linger on till the spring, when the new leaves push the old ones off.

Dad loved the autumn, or the 'Fall' as he learned to call it in America. It was his favourite season. As we followed a forest path I chatted to him about my new job with the

European Commission. He understood why I wanted to work for Europe. That day, as we trod on the fallen leaves, I realised that, for the first time, Dad was not keeping up with me. He looked grey and seemed out of breath.

Whenever we travelled to Ballybradden, after we had been given our tea, Dad would announce that we would walk 'the marches'. He would lead us out to inspect the fields where the farm ended, and to look at the lie of the land beyond. Borrowing Wellington boots to protect us from the muddy lanes, we would walk to the farthest reaches of the farm. Dad would stand at a corner of a field, or at the end of the back lane. Gazing into the distance, perhaps towards Gallows Hill or the Hurling Pitch, he would talk, with Uncle Robbie standing by his side.

Dad might say something to you when he was walking side by side that he wouldn't say to your face. Ulstermen of his generation, particularly countrymen, were hard to read. They did not show emotion or give sentimental speeches. Had they done so, their sons, raised in the same way, would have cringed. Praise was seldom given, and Dad was careful not to compliment one son more than the other.

However, on the day of my graduation from Edinburgh University, as we walked to the McEwan Hall, me dressed in a robe and hood, Dad, wearing his Edinburgh University sports tie, said to me:

'You know I'm as proud of you today as the day when you played in the Ulster Schools' Cup Final.'

That was a rare compliment. After the match in 1973 he had said nothing about my performance. He just told some story about how he met a pal of his in the stands, who had wondered which team he was supporting, to which Dad had replied that he 'had a lad on the pitch'.

Dad died suddenly of a massive heart attack on 18 February 1983. He collapsed outside the post office in Carryduff. Mum, who was standing close by, knew at once that he was gone.

In the days and months after his death I thought back to the words he uttered in Edinburgh. Thank God he said them. Otherwise I might still be unsure about how he really felt about me. I was never in doubt that my mother loved me. She told me often.

When you are young you may imagine a parent's death, and even relish the sad thoughts. The real thing was different. Dad's death hit me like a sledgehammer. It floored me. In the months afterwards I discovered emotions inside me, such as anger, that I had never felt before. I have never completely recovered from the shock. 'Dad, Dad,' I cried out, on the night he died, 'it was all for you. Ravenhill, Edinburgh, Dublin, Brussels – I got there for you.' I never had the chance to say those last words to him. By the time I read his last letter in Zaventem airport, on my way to the Ireland–France match for which he had once again found me a ticket, he was already dead.

The funeral service at Newtownbreda Church on the Ormeau Road was packed. John and I joined our arms round our shoulders, as did cousins James and John, and together we bore the coffin out of the church. I had never carried a coffin before. The load was so heavy that I was frightened that I might drop it. They must have been still making coffins out of solid wood, for Dad was not overweight when he died. As we walked unsteadily down the aisle, the tears streamed down my face. John managed to hold it together that day, but broke down a year later when asked to carry Uncle Robbie's coffin down the Ballybradden lane.

A few months after the funeral, Dad came to me in a dream. The two of us were together high above Northern Ireland, spread out below us like a map, or as you would see it from a plane arriving at Aldergrove airport. We walked side by side towards North Antrim and the hills he loved, the low range where Knockahollet marks the boundary between the fertile plain and the Glens of Antrim. Dad said to me, 'This is my country; these are my people', and we walked together through the land. It was a dream of great comfort. I wish it would recur to me, for dreams are the only place where I may walk with my father now.

PART FIVE

Echoes

2018-2023

Duke Street

As a traditional Presbyterian, I feel that a Sunday morning service is not complete without a Scottish metrical psalm. One stands out. The tune is 'Duke Street', and the psalm opens with the words 'Oh Lord, thou art my God and King'.

The beauty of the metrical psalms lies not only in their words, but also in the harmonies. In 'Duke Street' the bass line is as good a tune as the soprano, and it sometimes rises above it. I have sung this tune on memorable occasions – a wedding in St Giles Cathedral in Edinburgh, and also in the open air, as our covenanting forefathers might have done, outside an old kirk in Wigtownshire.

Dad loved 'Duke Street'. He had not been trained to sing, but he learnt this one bass line from listening to the music at Ballyweaney. Dad could not reach notes higher than the G below middle C. When the bass line rose above that he just sang the same note until the line returned down

| The Corncrake's Welcome

to his level again. In church his bass drone could be heard above the choir, amplified by the microphone in the pulpit.

I chose 'Duke Street' to be played at his funeral, as well as 'Hyfrydol', a tune that he loved listening to me playing on the piano. But when the time came to sing I could not do it. My voice died in my throat. Try as I might, no words came out.

Many years later, in 2010, I visited Belfast to see Mum, who was in a nursing home, after falling and breaking her hip. It was a Sunday and I plucked up the courage to go back to Windsor Presbyterian Church. I had not been inside the door since we left Belfast in 1975.

It was sad to see so few people, sitting singly in the pews, where once there had been a full congregation of young people and families. I recognised one or two old grey heads. I studied the list of praise but was disappointed that there were no psalms.

However, at the end of the sermon, the minister said, 'There is a change in the worship. Instead of the hymn on the order of service we will now sing "Oh Lord, thou art my God and King" to the tune "Duke Street".'

How did he know? Did he recognise me? Once more I could hardly sing the ancient uplifting tune.

When we first arrived in Donegal Dad played a trick on Mum. We were sitting at the dinner table one evening when he turned to Paola.

'Paola dear, if you were to look round this manse, what's the one thing you would add?'

Paola thought for a moment.

'You know, I think it maybe needs a piano.'

'Do you tell me that?'

The next time we visited St Johnston, Mum had bought a second-hand piano for the drawing room. Dad's psychology had worked. Paola told me that Dad had prepared the piano coup with her beforehand.

In the evenings in St Johnston I would sit at the piano playing. If I happened to play hymns and psalms, I would gradually become aware that the door to the room was ajar, and Dad was standing there.

Today it's exactly forty years since Dad died. I took out the old hymnbook and sang and played 'Duke Street' on the piano.

Closely Related to Chester

During my career, I came across many American diplomats, in different parts of the world. When I told them that I was Irish they were always friendly. A quarter of all US adults have Irish ancestors. What's more, twenty-three of the forty-six US presidents claim Irish heritage.

Standing at Fourth of July receptions at US embassies, watching the Stars and Stripes being unfurled, I have sometimes been tempted to reveal to an American colleague next to me a fact that Dad was immensely proud of: we are closely related to the twenty-first president of the United States of America.

The twenty-first sounds like a significant number. I would watch my American friend's eyes rise as he tried to guess which president I meant. Eventually I would put the poor fellow out of his embarrassment by revealing the name of my illustrious American relative: Chester Alan Arthur.

Most US diplomats have just about heard of my cousin Chester, which is more than can be said for the bulk of Americans. He usually tops the list of the least known and most obscure chief executives of the USA. Chester was a vice-president who took office in 1881 after President Garfield was assassinated. He never expected to be president. He was just the other guy on the presidential ticket.

Chester Arthur was a Republican, known as a crooked crony of the New York party machine, and many people feared the worst when he took office. However, as Scott Greenberger has shown in a biography entitled *The Unexpected President*, once Chester Arthur assumed the highest office in the land he turned over a new leaf.

> 'He proved to be not just honest but brave, going up against the very forces that had controlled him for decades. He surprised everyone when he swept house and took on corruption, civil rights for blacks, and issues of land for Native Americans.'

James McGrath Morris has written that Chester Arthur's rise above politics could be a model for our age. Certainly, after the events of the last few years, culminating in the storming of the Capitol in January 2020, Chester A Arthur can no longer be considered the worst US president. He deserves to be rehabilitated. The slogan could be MAGA – Make Arthur Great Again.

Among the Savages

It was Dad who prompted my interest in our family history, but it was Miss Strahan who first stimulated my interest in British history. She gave me a prize for knowing the names and dates of the kings and queens of England. These started with 1066 and William the Conqueror, who became my first eponymous hero. *1066 and All That*, a spoof on British history, written in 1930, was one of Dad's favourite books. He loved the examination instruction '*do not on any account attempt to write on both sides of the paper at once*'.

In *Voyages with My Grandfather*, I researched my maternal grandparents, the Boyds and Higginsons. For this book I've tried to find out more about Dad's family, looking through the family Bible, and at websites, and spending an afternoon in a heritage centre in Dumfries in south-west Scotland.

Hanna is a Scots name. The family is originally from Wigtownshire in Galloway. The clan was powerful in the 16th century, and they built a castle at New Sorbie, sadly now a ruin. The Hannas declined in the early 17th century after a dispute with their rivals, the Murrays. In 1609 a group of Hannas killed one of the Murrays. The crime was committed on a Sabbath day, which made it worse. The fertile Hanna lands were taken away and the family was outlawed. Many of the clan who took to the hills were Covenanters. They were persecuted in the second part of the 17th century, and many went into exile to Ulster and on to America.

Today the Hanna name in America does not only come from Scotland. In 1996 we visited a Hanna winery in California, and discovered that the owner, Dr Hanna was originally from Syria. When I later visited Egypt, I found out that Hanna is a well-known surname throughout the Middle East. The immigration officer in Cairo who examined my passport smiled and said, 'Ah, Mr Hanna. How long are you coming home for?'

John had a theory about our family's oriental connection. He kept our copy of the Hanna crest in his room. It includes a cross above a crescent, a link with the Crusades. John thought that Gilbert aHanney, the crusader in question, could be a common Hanna ancestor, giving rise to both Middle Eastern and Scottish branches of the family.

Intriguing as the theory sounds, DNA research has not shown matches between Ulster-Scot Hannas and our Middle Eastern homonyms. My own DNA has been tested as 80% Scottish/Irish, with another 12% coming from the

Baltic and Norway, and a smidgeon from Spain. The Viking part is not unexpected, given their domination of the west of Scotland and of Ireland for many centuries. I wonder who was responsible for the Mediterranean part. Perhaps soldiers in the Spanish Armada of 1588, shipwrecked off the North Antrim coast, were given shelter by one of my ancestors.

Three of my four grandparents – Hannas, Pattersons and Boyds – came from rural Ulster-Scot families, tracing their origins to Galloway and Ayrshire. We don't know in what year their ancestors crossed the Narrow Sea to Ulster, but it was most likely at the end of the 17th century, maybe at the time of a famine in Scotland that lasted for seven years.

Unfortunately the records of the direct lines of these grandparents peter out after four or five generations. However, we know much more about my fourth grandparent Annie Higginson's family. The Higginsons are a long-established family that can trace lineage in Ireland back to the early 17th century, when Colonel Edward Higginson married Mary Savage of the Ards. Her family were seneschals of Ulster. One of them had the magnificent name of Juanico le bui Savage. He and his brother were killed in a battle with the O'Neills in 1603. According to their family history, Savages fought at the Battle of the Boyne in 1690 – on both sides, for William of Orange and for King James. Their ancestor William le Sauvage was a Norman knight who accompanied John de Courcy when he conquered Ulster in the 12th century. With some more research, perhaps one of my grandchildren will be able to connect our family directly to William the Conqueror, 1066 and all that. But maybe they should not attempt to write on both sides of the page at once...

Covenanters (ii)

In the summer after lockdown I visited Orkney for the first time. I was desperate to feel free. I wanted to see the birds for which Orkney is famous, and to explore two family connections with the islands. The first is that Orkney was obtained from Norway in 1468 by Lord Robert Boyd, who negotiated a marriage with James III of Scotland for Margaret, daughter of the King of Norway. The second concerns the Covenanters' Memorial.

Dad described in his memoirs how in the 1930s his family left the Covenanter tradition and its Reformed Presbyterian Church and joined the Presbyterian Church.

Covenanters were so called because they made a covenant never to renounce their religious beliefs. They opposed hierarchy in the church, rejecting bishops and the King who appointed them. They acknowledged only 'Christ the King'. This brought them into conflict with the

Stuart dynasty, who proclaimed the 'Divine Right of Kings'. After the restoration of Charles II in 1660, Covenanters were persecuted. Many died in what was called 'The Killing Time'. Sir Walter Scott's novel *Old Mortality*, set in that time, describes how they rebelled and the price they paid.

In 1679, a rebellion by Covenanters was quashed at the Battle of Bothwell Brig, near Kilmarnock. After the battle, 1,200 prisoners were taken to Edinburgh and herded into the open space at Greyfriars Church. Those who recanted their beliefs and accepted the rule of bishops were set free. Those who did not compromise were executed or died of illness or their wounds. By November, just over 200 diehards were left. One of these was Samuel Hannah, from Wigtown.

The remaining Covenanters were handed over to a sea captain who undertook to transport them as slaves to the plantations of America. Piled deep into the hold of the *Crown of London*, moored at the port of Leith, they were starved and left in miserable conditions before they embarked on their final voyage. A storm arose around Orkney. The captain anchored the ship off Deerness. During the night the ship broke its anchor and was dashed against the rocks. The captain and crew escaped by cutting down the mast and clambering along it to the shore. However, the captain refused to unlock the ship's hold, leaving the 200 Covenanters to their fate. He knew that he would be paid for prisoners delivered to the colonies, or for those who died on the voyage, but would receive nothing for anyone he released.

We visited Deerness on a midsummer's day. Our car was the only vehicle in the car park. We walked down a grassy lane to the monument. Curlews rose up and hovered over the buttercup-filled meadows, protecting their young with plaintive cries. A pair of oystercatchers escorted us, lest we venture off the beaten path and disturb their nests. One peeped from a fence post, while the other waddled along the path in front of us.

The Covenanters' memorial is a grey-stone tower, erected by public subscription at the end of the 19th century. No names are engraved on the monument.

The day was bright; the sky was blue. I looked down the cliff to the water's edge a hundred feet below, where the sea was calm. Little waves broke over the basalt blocks on which the *Crown of London* had foundered. I imagined a stormy night and the Covenanters down below, captive beneath the battened hatches of the boat.

My eyes were filled with the sight of sea birds – razorbills, guillemots, shags and a pair of puffins. A weather-beaten notice explained that most of the Covenanters were drowned, but a few managed to escape. Some members of the crew took pity on them and released them. Some who struggled ashore were again arrested and ended up in Jamaica. Others stayed in Orkney, and a few may have made it to Holland or Ireland.

We walked across the headland to Mull Point, and came across a colony of fulmars, some nesting on rocky perches while others patrolled, fast and low along the cliff-edge, like fighter pilots trying to ward off the raids of the merciless great skuas.

As we walked back across the headland, I thought of the Covenanters who survived 'The Killing Time'. Sir Walter Scott describes them as a fearful lot, prone to splitting into narrower sects whenever disputes arose among them. They handed down their genes to Northern Irish Protestants. These included my grandfather's uncle, John Carlisle, who enjoyed arguing about religious doctrine and abhorred any innovations. He drank heavily, but, as my grandfather remembered, *'never paid for it on the Sabbath day'*. And there was the Covenanting Minister of Kilraughts who denounced my father's family from the pulpit because his two uncles had fought 'for King and Country' in the First World War. One of them, Samuel Patterson, was killed at the Somme. Their father – my great-grandfather James Patterson – walked out of the church on that Sabbath day, never to return. I've recently learnt where Samuel Patterson's grave lies in France. We must go there and remember him too.

Partners

Gail Walker, past editor of the *Belfast Telegraph*, interviewed me in 2020 about *Voyages with My Grandfather*. She was interested in my stories about Uncle Jack and the Second World War and in Uncle Robin's work as a codebreaker. She was also curious about Windsor Manse and the life of a clergyman's family. She wanted to know why I had written the book, and she noticed that Anne Louise had died young.

'That must have been hard,' she said.

For a moment I couldn't speak. I hadn't talked to anyone about Anne Louise for many years. It took me a while to tell Gail that Anne Louise died of cancer at the age of twenty-seven. This was in 1985, two years after Dad's death.

When we were children, Anne Louise was a tomboy, wearing jeans and Aran pullovers, trying to imitate her older brothers. When the Troubles were at their height, my parents sent her to boarding school in England. She went there a stringy teenager and returned an elegant young woman. She spent a year looking after children in Edinburgh and a year in Italy, staying with Paola's cousins in Rome. Maybe she spent too long in the sun. She had inherited Mum's wafer-thin Irish skin.

Anne Louise was happily married to John, born on the same day as me. She was training to be a nurse in Southampton. One day she discovered a mole on her upper arm. It was at the back where she did not see it soon enough. Cancer was diagnosed and it spread rapidly. She died within a year.

What can I say about my lost sister? She was a beautiful girl, with lovely dimples. She was tall, wore her hair short, and looked like Princess Diana. We called her and Dad the partners. She used to trim his hair. She was a good person, who cared about other people.

All during Anne Louise's illness Mum was with her, holding her hand, persuading inexperienced health staff to allow her to die at home. I was downstairs in her house when I heard her leave this world. It was heart-wrenching. It shouldn't have been Mum nursing her, but her nursing Mum in old age. She would have looked after Mum better than I could.

I wish it hadn't been this way. I loved Andy dearly. Would that she had been spared to share in our lives, to have children and grow older with us. I would love to have a sister to talk to today. It was not to be. I hold her in my heart, forever young.

JRBH

———

These days I wear two rings. On the left hand I have my wedding ring and on the right hand a signet ring that Mum gave John for his 21st birthday. It has his initials engraved – JRBH for John Robert Boyd Hanna. I found it abandoned and broken in John's flat and had it repaired by a jeweller in Brussels. The faded initials remind me of John and the Boyd Hanna family connection.

John was in the year above me at school. He was always taller – at one stage, when we were adolescents, by six inches, later by just an inch. But in many ways we were like twins. We both attended Inchmarlo and Inst, where we both were in the top stream. Then one day, when he was fifteen years of age, John went mad. Before that he was just John. After that he was my crazy brother John.

In 1969 we went on a family holiday to Denmark. We took our car, a green Corsair, and toured the country, stopping at pre-paid hotels. John and I were teenagers, becoming too big and awkward for a family holiday. For the first time I could sense tension in our family. Mum and Dad had to watch their money, kept in travellers' cheques, and complain when hotel owners added extra charges. Dad was hopeless at protesting. He was too kind, always seeing the other person's point of view. Mum was sharper. They didn't always see eye to eye. John and I were embarrassed by our parents and happy to return home to Belfast.

In August John's O level results came through. He had obtained five grade 1s, which was outstanding – he was one of the best in his year. Academic success seemed to set John off in a new direction. Early in the autumn term of his lower sixth year he began to have wild mood swings. He listened more and more to heavy blues music, played as loud as possible. He started painting his room. The wallpaper had green, yellow and black dots on a white background, but he covered it brown – all brown – from floor to ceiling, working at it all through the night. He couldn't stop and he couldn't sleep. Day after day, night after night, he stayed awake. He stayed home from school. A doctor was called in and gave him sedatives.

One day John discovered the solution to the political problems of Northern Ireland, and decided to go to London to tell Jim Callaghan, the prime minister. He upped and left for the boat, without telling anyone, and with no money. The police found him wandering round Belfast Harbour and phoned Mum and Dad to collect him. Another time he shaved off all his hair, amazing his classmates, who nicknamed him 'Skinhead'. He spent long periods in the

City Hospital and in Purdysburn Hospital. He underwent several sessions of electric shock treatment. I remember seeing him after the treatment, looking like a zombie. His brain had been shaken to pieces. God knows what damage was done. It still pains me to think of it.

At first we were told that John had had a nervous breakdown. Later the diagnosis was manic depression, now called bipolar disease. There is no real cure. Medication can help, although the side effects of many years of taking lithium are severe. The bipolar gene comes from Dad's side of the family. An uncle who suffered from it spent much of his life drinking in the Pound, the local pub in Loughgiel. Our cousin Roy was also a sufferer, and, like John, was in and out of hospital, sometimes taking his medication and sometimes not.

Dad had no idea of how to deal with John and his illness. It was Mum who called for doctors and went on rescue missions to extract him from a tangle when a manic episode took hold of him and he went on a spending spree. He once bought a yellow Jaguar, which he never drove.

In spite of his illness, John obtained a university degree in chemistry and worked for nine years at the Linen Research Centre in Lambeg. He led conservation groups and worked at the Ulster Museum. Transcendental meditation gave him some peace of mind. During the week he lived in sheltered accommodation off the Lisburn Road, and at the weekend he helped Mum out at Carryduff. He often came on holiday with us to Ballycastle and loved being with his nephew and nieces. He wrote many drafts of novels, in the style of Flann O'Brien. After John died in 2017, I found this poem, unpublished until now:

BOW TIE

Presbyterian software fits the bill
Clouds of cognisance climb
where scorpions saluted promising
bundles of hayloft material.
Popular programmes get a massive response
of undetected litter bugs.

Momentarily surrender is achieved by the nodding
tails of noxious charismatic club leaders.
Under the clouds, sirens blare out a message
Of badly mismanaged hoopla games.
Protestant ethics are triply by-passed
as minute offerings are collected.

Balloons multiply skywards occasionally.
Scaffolding sometimes shows signs of collusion
between builder and owner as if catastrophic
subterranean mustard gas, introduced when
nobody had least expected it

British, Irish or Both

In 1995 an Anglo-Irish Agreement was reached, and in 1997 the Good Friday Agreement put an end to almost thirty years of violence in Northern Ireland. The new agreements used the same formula of power-sharing as the ill-fated Sunningdale Agreement of 1973. As the deputy SDLP leader Seamus Mallon said, the Good Friday Agreement was 'Sunningdale for slow learners'.

The Good Friday Agreement has been observed for twenty-five years. Today a generation has grown up that doesn't remember the bombing and killing, the terror, 'the years of disgrace', as the poet Michael Longley has named them. Those who were injured and those who lost loved ones can never be consoled. Their suffering must not be forgotten. But Northern Ireland was given the chance to move on.

There are many different elements in the Agreement,

including the release of prisoners, decommissioning of arms and complex political structures. One simple provision delighted me most:

'People born in Northern Ireland may identify themselves as Irish or British or both.'

In the past, when people asked me where I was from, I always replied 'Belfast'. I didn't say where Belfast was, because to do so might label me according to nationality or religion. I didn't want to be classified in this way. Now I was being given a choice of three identities. At last there was an advantage in being born in Belfast, something that made us special.

This provision was inspired and liberating. The physical border between Northern Ireland and the Republic was progressively disappearing within the EU. The border in people's minds could also vanish, should they allow it to. The Good Friday Agreement, with backing from Ireland, the UK, the USA and the EU, gave people wherever they came from in Northern Ireland, whatever their religious background, the right to feel at home, to belong, and not to be considered strangers or second-class citizens.

What is our identity today? Irish, British or both? Some people think of themselves as Northern Irish. I see myself as an Ulster-Scot. We are also European, whether we are part of the EU or not. If we could only realise that we have a rich inheritance, made up of many threads, and many identities, the differences between us could simply disappear, as when the sea mists rise from the Causeway Coast on a summer's day to reveal the beauty of Fair Head, and beyond it the Mull of Kintyre.

Dublin Revisited

After retiring from the European External Action Service, I returned to Dublin twice. On 14 August 2018, forty years to the day after I had joined the Irish Foreign Service, I retraced my steps across St Stephen's Green to Iveagh House. How Dublin had changed in that time. When the bus from the airport entered a new tunnel I was surprised to emerge ten minutes later into a brand new city beside the River Liffey. The old tenements, topped by towering TV aerials to capture BBC and ITV broadcasts, had disappeared and were replaced by block after block of modern buildings, the financial quarter.

The transformation of Dublin was breathtaking. In the 1960s the Republic of Ireland was poorer and less developed than the industrial North. Northerners tended to look down on it. Dublin, once the second city of the British Empire, seemed quaint and old-fashioned. When

I left in 1981, Ireland was still one of the poorest member states of the EEC. However, things changed. By the turn of the century, thanks to decades of access to the European Single Market, US investment, and the education and dynamism of its young people, Ireland had become the Celtic Tiger, one of the richest European countries. Ireland had experienced one of the most remarkable and fastest transformations of any country in the world.

In 2007, when I was serving as EU ambassador to Uruguay, a British member of the European Parliament, part of a delegation visiting Latin America, asserted in front of the Uruguayan parliament that no European country had ever benefitted from membership of the European Union. This surprised Uruguayan MPs who knew about the democratic and economic progress of member states such as Spain after they joined the EU. Many Uruguayans were eager to emulate the European Union by integrating their own region of Mercosur (Brazil, Argentina, Uruguay and Paraguay).

My job was to promote closer relations between Uruguay and the EU, and to encourage regional integration, and I could not let the MEP's statement go unchallenged. I took the microphone and said that that I knew of a small European country, about the size of Uruguay, which had started off as one of the poorest member states of the EU, and was now one of the richest. The MEP, a charming person, seemed puzzled by my remarks. 'But I thought you were British.'

That same MEP and other unscrupulous British journalists and politicians spun false stories about the EU in the British press for over twenty-five years, often finding it convenient to blame 'Brussels' for problems that were a national responsibility. In 2016, using new methods of targeted disinformation, and playing on fears of migration, they conned voters into forfeiting European freedoms – the free movement of people, goods, services and capital – that they had enjoyed for over forty years. Brexit closed the UK off from its closest trading partners and neighbours, reduced the UK's influence in Europe and in the world, and made it a less attractive location for investment. It was a colossal act of collective folly. Today, seven years after the vote, many UK citizens realise the damage their choice has inflicted on themselves and their country, and how it has brought back to the surface problems that had been resolved in Ireland.

In 2018, while the new financial quarter of Dublin was visible for all to see, on the far side of the Liffey, Georgian Dublin – Trinity, Grafton Street and St Stephen's Green – remained as charming as ever, and more populated by young people. On Grafton Street I had coffee in Bewley's. On Leeson Street I drank a pint of Guinness in the pub I went to in 1980 on the day Luisa was born.

All was not rosy in Ireland during the years of change. Corruption and cronyism were rampant, and the benefits of the economic miracle were not evenly spread. The financial system came crashing down in 2008. Fintan O'Toole has written of Ireland during these years, and of how behind a façade there was hypocrisy and repression, in which the Catholic Church played a cruel role.

I recall the Belvedere College Rugby team who came to Belfast to play against us at under-14 level. They had a dashing centre who scored twice in the first half. At half-time I overheard their coach, a priest dressed in a flowing cassock, admonishing the boy for not passing the ball to another player, saying that he would take him off the pitch if he scored again. The boy did score a third try and the priest immediately implemented his threat. At the time I admired the iron discipline of the priest but felt sorry for the talented boy. We know today that some priests abused their power and abused many boys at schools throughout the land, including in the elite rugby-playing schools.

There was a funnier incident a few years later, when we were playing against Blackrock College in Dublin and they were running rings round us. At one point I glared at my opposite number, as rugby forwards sometimes do, when the boy's mother, dressed in a leopard skin coat, ran onto the pitch and hit me over the head with an umbrella. I was surprised but unharmed. I wonder if the boy remembers his mother's embarrassing pitch invasion on his behalf.

My Pilgrim Journey

My second post-retirement visit to Dublin was not planned. I had been playing golf in Dunfanaghy, County Donegal, and was on my way back to Brussels. Arriving at Dublin airport I learnt that thunderstorms in Belgium prevented my flight from taking off. It was postponed for twenty-four hours. I helped an ancient Argentinian couple to understand what was going on, translating Aer Lingus English into Rioplatense Spanish, and joined them for more conversation over a dubious dinner, courtesy of our national airline. A bus took us to a hotel in Tallaght for the night.

Next morning, as I stood at a bus stop, wondering what to do with the unexpected gift of a day in Dublin, a lady suggested that I visit Trinity College to see the Books of Kells. *Why not?* I thought. I took the bus to Nassau Street and queued up for a tour of the College, given by an undergraduate. The highlight was the visit of the library, containing one of the world's most beautiful and precious books, the 9th century Bible, transcribed by monks in Iona and illuminated with Celtic designs.

What to do next, with an afternoon to kill before going to the airport?

I had seen one of the most famous books in the world, but there was another little-known book on my list. Dublin could be just the right place to find out more about a man who was born, like Dad, in Loughgiel, Co Antrim around the same time, and who rose to the highest level in the Catholic Church in Ireland, Cardinal Cahal Daly. I had discovered that Cahal Daly had written an autobiography, and I was curious to compare his recollections with Dad's.

Fred Hanna's bookshop, for many years a landmark on Nassau Street, had disappeared. Most Dubliners ask me if I'm related to Fred Hanna, which I am not. We Irish are always looking to establish a connection through names and places. I found another bookshop further up the street. The sales assistant was able to find out the title of Daly's book, *Steps on My Pilgrim Journey*, but the bookshop did not stock it. They suggested that I might find a copy at the Cloister Bookshop in Lower Abbey Street.

So I continued my literary tour around Dublin, a Joycean perambulation through the city, stopping for a pint at one of the writer's favourite pubs, walking across O'Connell Bridge, pausing for coffee, and ending up at the Cloister Bookshop, which specialised in holy books, as well as candles and other religious artefacts. Inside the bookshop, assistants moved about in a hushed way, like librarians in a seminary. I found a pamphlet about Cardinal Daly, but not his autobiography. However, the shop manager knew of the book. He decided to search in the basement, where at last he found a copy, a thick blue hardback, which he sold to me for the reasonable price of five euros.

That evening, on the flight to Brussels, I opened Cardinal Daly's book and was astounded. Not only was Cahal Daly born in the same village as Dad, but he came from the same townland, Ballybradden. And there, in the opening pages, was Dad's name:

"Several Protestant families had sons studying for the ministry as I was studying for the priesthood and I formed friendships with many of these, friendships which were maintained throughout later life and were greatly cherished. They included Reverend William Hanna, Presbyterian, later minister of Randalstown O.C. and then of Windsor."

Reading these pages brought back to me the evening in 1983 when I opened Dad's last weekly letter at Brussels airport, and read of his hope that peace would one day return to Ireland.

The Sky Ablaze (ii)

Cahal Daly was granted a longer life than Dad, living into his nineties. A teacher of philosophy, a clear-thinking writer, he admired the theology of non-violence developed by Gandhi and Martin Luther King. Although he kept it hidden at the time, it was he who drafted the speeches for Pope John Paul II's visit to Ireland in 1979. The appeal to the extremists, *'On my knees I beg you to turn away from the path of violence'*, that resonates down the years, came from Cahal Daly's heart and pen.

Cahal Daly rejected violence throughout his career. He supported John Hume in the talks with Sinn Féin that led to the peace process. As a Catholic cardinal he visited the US together with Protestant clergymen. Alongside Anglican Primate Robert Eames and the then Presbyterian Moderator John Dunlop, Cardinal Daly worked tirelessly for peace and helped the process that eventually led to the Peace Agreement.

Daly was writing his memoirs during the first week of May 1998, just after the signing of the Good Friday Agreement. He hoped then that, '*by God's grace we could be close to the formal ending of the longest campaign of insurgency in our island history, and at the beginning of the healing of one of Europe's longest-lasting and most bitter conflicts – that between Ireland and Britain and between Irish and British traditions in Ireland itself.*'

Cahal Daly gained credibility among Protestants for the hard line he took about IRA activity. He was forthright and unambiguous in condemning violence from his own community as well as from the other side. How was it that he took such a stance, when some other Catholic clergy had been ambivalent?

From his memoirs I learnt that Daly's attitude stemmed back to an event that occurred when he was a child. Born in 1917, just a year after Dad, his earliest memory, from a winter's night in 1921, was of being held in his father's arms in his night attire, outside his house in Ballybradden, pointing up at the roof, and asking, in whatever words he then knew, 'Who lit the living-room fire up on the roof of the house?'

The four-year-old child Daly did not know what was happening. The house he lived in was a double house with the Loughgiel Police Barracks next door. The IRA had decided to burn it down, as part of its nationwide operations. That night his parents and their four children were burnt out of their house and lost all their possessions. Fifty years later Daly met one of the IRA men who took part in the operation and who lifted him out of his cradle and carried him outside, after ordering his parents to evacuate the house in great haste.

I wonder if Cahal Daly ever knew – did Dad ever tell him? – that the next morning a small Protestant boy on his way to church, in a pony and trap, saw the burning embers of the house beside the police barracks, and also wondered what on earth was going on.

How amazing, and yet understandable, that when the two boys from Loughgiel separately recorded their memoirs, each of them started with the fire across the fields, the blazing barracks branded onto their infant brains. One was an innocent victim, and the other a helpless spectator. One was a Catholic and one a Protestant. Both later became clergymen and peace-makers. Their shared childhood experience of the events of 1921 led them to oppose violence in any shape or form, and to make it their life's work to preach peace, tolerance and good neighbourliness.

In the 1970s and '80s, when he had become a bishop, Cahal Daly, like Dad, often had to visit the homes and pray with families of those who had just lost loved ones. Daly wrote *'there is a common human heartbreak, there are universal human tears in all these tragedies and they have no political and religious colouring: nationalist tears and loyalist tears are indistinguishable.'* I'm sure Dad would have agreed.

One of the pamphlets I bought at the Cloister Bookshop was a series of tributes to Cardinal Daly from leaders of both communities in Northern Ireland. It closes with a poem by Rev. Ruth Patterson, the first woman to become a minister in the Presbyterian Church in Ireland. Her father, Rev. Tom Patterson, was a good friend of Dad's, and also met the Pope in 1979. Ruth kindly gave me permission to reproduce her poem here.

In the cold hardness of winter you left us.
Frozen earth – unyielding, journeying hazardous,
A blanket of snow hiding ugliness and beauty alike,
Presenting us with an unreal world,
Masking hidden dangers for all would-be pilgrims

You knew the dangers, yet stepped out fearlessly, but with
*   humility,*
Passionately walking the road towards justice and peace,
Naming the ugliness of violence and division,
Proclaiming always the beauty of the Kingdom that is real
And all about us, that unseen world for us still hidden,
But now, for you, reality.

In the cold hardness of political impasse you left us,
A peace process endessly frozen
Barely masking the ugliness of power and control,
Of violence unaddressed, of sectarianism undiminished.
Calling into question the beauty of unity in diversity,
Of hospitality restored, and room enough for all.
Yet people must still hope for spring and resurrection

Join with us as we pray
We who take such stumbling steps on our pilgrim journey,
That after the cold hardness of winter,
Our frozen hearts will melt and a new spring,
A new beginning, a new day will dawn
For Ireland, church and world.

I often look at the photo of Dad meeting the Pope.
Recently I've noticed a hand stretched out towards my

father from someone standing in the shadow of the pontiff. I like to think that it is Cahal Daly's hand, and that he is saying to the Pope, *'This is Bill Hanna. We are from the same village in the North of Ireland. Although he is a Protestant, we have always been the best of friends.'*

The Corncrake's
Welcome (ii)

Over the last twenty years our family has regrouped in Scotland. David studied, like his parents, at Edinburgh University, and stayed on in the city. Later Emilia arrived to work in Edinburgh, and today both children and three grandchildren live here. Luisa and our three other grandchildren live in Sheffield, not so very far away. When I think back to four generations of family connections with Edinburgh, it seems the right place to be. Here I also feel close to Ireland.

In one of his first addresses to the good folk of St Johnston, Dad talked of the beauty of the moon shining over the River Foyle. An eyebrow or two was raised, as the congregation wondered what sort of romantic fellow they had chosen as their new pastor. However, it is not unknown for a Presbyterian minister to wax lyrical. WR

Rodgers, a Presbyterian clergyman in County Armagh, and contemporary of Louis MacNeice, wrote some of the most romantic, and even erotic, poetry in the Northern Irish canon. Dad didn't go that far.

Dad delighted in his rediscovery of the Ulster countryside. He would roll off the names of the townlands of his beloved County Antrim – Loughgiel, Ballybradden and Drumabest – before naming those he had recently discovered in County Donegal – Taughboyne, Teentamucklagh, and Classeygowan. He loved to bring visual aids into the pulpit. Brandishing a flail for winnowing corn, he would capture everyone's attention with a flourish. Often he talked of the birds he saw, the swans and geese flying in formation over the Foyle. He accompanied their flight with his arms widespread and his black robes billowing.

One of his children's addresses was entitled 'Crex Crex', the Latin name for the corncrake. He began by showing a wooden rattle of the sort then used to make noise at football matches and known in Ireland as a 'corncrake'. No doubt he gave it a good shake to wake up any of the congregation who had dozed off. He told of how a former viceroy of Ireland, living in his Dublin residence, used to complain that he couldn't sleep because of the din of the corncrakes. Policemen were detailed to spend all night chasing away the noisy birds from their hideouts in the long grass at Phoenix Park.

The corncrake, like the swallow, is an African migrant. It had been common when Dad was a boy. However, by the 1970s, with the widespread use of the combine harvester, the bird had all but disappeared from the Irish countryside.

'*But good news,*' Dad announced to his parishioners. '*The corncrakes are coming back to Ireland. Yes, some of them are already here. The corncrake has been heard this year in Shannon Harbour, Kilkee, Kinsale, Ballina, Kells Bay and Lisnaskea in County Fermanagh. And this year, on 6 June, up there just outside Dunfanaghy I heard it myself. No less than three times. Three long corncrake songs in a field close beside me. Girls and boys, I am so glad the birds of the air are often mentioned in the Bible. Lord Jesus often talked about the birds. Some of them have a hoarse voice like the corncrake, and some have a lovely singing voice, like the blackbird or the nightingale, but they all remind you and me that we should keep on praising God, with whatever voice we have.*'

Last year we travelled to the island of Uist, in the Outer Hebrides, where they have been reintroducing the corncrake. To protect the birds, farmers have agreed not to mow their meadows until late summer. The project has had some success. Local folk told me I would be able to hear the corncrake at a nearby field. Every day for a fortnight I walked up the road to the field, full of nettles. However, I was disappointed: I saw curlews and terns nesting on the machair but heard nothing of the *Crex crex*.

At length I abandoned my search for the elusive bird, and went to play golf at Askernish, at the southern end of Uist. The course was designed in the 1890s by old Tom Morris, the architect of many famous links courses, including Rosapenna in Donegal and St Andrews in Fife. Set in the natural environment of the sand dunes, Askernish was neglected for many years and was only recently rediscovered and brought back into play. No earth-moving equipment was required to restore its glory. All it took was a man with a lawnmower, and the skills of the 19th-century golf-course designer were once more revealed.

I relished the springy turf, carpeted with wild-flowers – daisies, bird's-foot-trefoil, and eyebright – and the larks rising up from the fairways, '*singing and soaring, soaring and singing*', to paraphrase the poet. One spectacular hole, a 200-yard par 3, looks over a valley to the island of Barra to the south. The drive was straight into the wind, and I was exhilarated when my ball reached the green safely. I thought it as stunning a view, and as stern a test of golf, as the famous 'Calamity' at Royal Portrush.

Paola joined me at Askernish on the first day, but after that I was on my own. Except that I am never entirely alone when I'm walking on a links course. There are so many birds to enjoy, and I occasionally glimpse Dad too, dressed in his old sky-blue pullover, bending over a putt, with a wooden tee stuck between his teeth, or clipping a 4-wood along the fairway.

At the end of my round, I loaded my golf clubs into the car and set off down the lane, with fenced meadows on either side. I had gone about a hundred yards when a red light on the dashboard alerted me that the back door was not properly shut. I stopped and got out to close it. Just as I was getting back into the driving seat a sound came from somewhere in the long grass of a meadow, about twenty yards away. It was tuneless and repetitive, like a comb being played on your fingers, a noise such as I had never heard before, but which brought a tear to my eye. When it stopped abruptly I wondered if I had just imagined it.

Two days later I visited Askernish once more. At the end of my round of golf I stopped the car at the same spot on the lane, and, sure enough, heard the same sound. Two women were walking along the road. I asked them if I had heard correctly. 'Oh yes,' one replied. 'That's the corncrake. We often hear it hereabouts.'

It's true that the corncrake is not melodious. Nor, if you chance to see it – I didn't – is it much to look at. It has none of the majesty of the white-tailed eagle we photographed on the same holiday. Over the years I have been privileged to observe rarer birds, such as the weird-looking picathartes in Ghana. But the *Crex crex* in Uist was, I think, the most comforting bird-song I have ever heard. I had been waiting more than half my life to hear it.

My Belfast

When Kenneth Branagh's film *Belfast* came out last year I saw it with the family. I was eager to see how Branagh would portray my home city, and how my family would react.

The opening shots, in colour, show today's Belfast, with its twin Goliath cranes and the gleaming Titanic museum. But the colour soon fades away, and we are taken back to the black and white world of Belfast in 1969.

We are at the beginning of the Troubles, a time of rioting and intimidation. People are being burned out of their houses. We see, through a child's eyes, what it is like to grow up in an ever more dangerous city. The film is about loss – about the time before the Troubles when there was a sense of family and community in Belfast. And who other than Van Morrison, our own nostalgic and grumpy genius, to provide the soundtrack.

When my nine-year-old grandson heard the clergyman preaching a hellfire sermon, he asked if my father was like that in the pulpit. I told him that his great-grandfather never guldered in our church on the Lisburn Road. We were brought up on a diet of sermons, but the messages were kind and delivered gently. We were taught about right and wrong, not about damnation and condemnation.

The conflict Branagh shows in North Belfast is not so much between Catholics and Protestants as about decent people trying to stand up against the hard men – who will soon become paramilitaries – on their own side. These are the men who tell Branagh's father to *'participate or pay'.* Over in South Belfast, my father was preaching a gospel of love and good neighbourliness. The more the violence took hold, the more Dad preached against it. I was proud of him.

A few days after seeing the film I travelled to Northern Ireland. I sailed into Belfast on a sunny morning and from the Lough I saw the emblematic cranes. I soon found myself at Oxford Street bus station, scene of one of the worst bombs on Bloody Friday, July 1972. I had my first summer job nearby, working for the *News Letter*, and was supposed to go into the city that afternoon to collect my pay. Luckily for me I heard the first of the twenty bomb blasts echo across the city just as I was about to set out and stayed safely at home.

The bus station has long since been rebuilt, but as I walked along the High Street, through the most ancient part of Belfast, for a moment or two I had the old reflex of scanning faces to spot the potential bomber. I turned into Ann Street, past where the Abercorn used to be. That was one of the first and most shocking bombs, planted by the IRA. Scores of city shoppers, on a Saturday afternoon, many of them women, were cut to pieces by debris and exploding glass from the popular tea-room. The cruelty and senselessness of it all.

In 1972 whole swathes of Belfast were blown apart. But whereas Branagh had to recreate his street on a film set, my part of Belfast, the Windsor district, looks today much as it was back then. Our area was safer than most, but we also had our share of violence: as well as the bomb at Stewarts Supermarket, there were shootings at St Brigid's Catholic Church at the far end of Derryvolgie Avenue.

I drove up the Lisburn Road and parked in Malone Avenue. I walked past the little hall where on Sunday afternoons we used to attend Crusaders. Today it has become the Belfast Spiritual Church. Across the road, Windsor Park, the Northern Ireland football ground, remains, three hundred yards away from Windsor Manse. From our attic we could glimpse a corner of the pitch and one goalpost. Looking through binoculars, on the day of an international, I once had a free view of George Best playing, but only during the first half when he ventured down the left wing.

Over the road at the manse, the lime trees where John and I used to climb up and hide in summer were bald. Next to the Malone Telephone Exchange, where two Japanese cherry trees have been replaced by tarmacadam, was the spot my mother and Anne Louise chose for family photos. A sign on the red-brick wall called for Julian Assange to be freed. The manse was sold many years ago to the Peace People, who also urged passers-by to 'Cut carbon *and abolish militarism and the war industry*. The disused telephone exchange has recently been converted into penthouse flats. I wonder what the new occupants think of the messages next door.

Unfortunately the writing was also on the wall for Windsor Presbyterian Church – around which my life revolved for my first twenty years.

I thought back to the time when Dad organised an ecumenical service with our Catholic neighbours. Protestant fundamentalists disapproved and organised a bomb scare. The police and the army arrived. While John and I peeked out of his bedroom window, protected by Sellotape, and watched the army deploy a new-fangled robot, the service was relocated to St Brigid's Catholic Church, where it went ahead as planned. The robot advanced to the boot of the car, blew it open, but no great explosion followed. The bomb scare proved to have been a hoax, and our church was left unscathed.

However, forty more years of Northern Irish weather took a heavy toll on the sandstone Victorian structure. Repairs to the massive building, with its tall spire, proved too costly for the congregation, which was forced to abandon the building. Soon after my visit, the last Sunday worship in Windsor Presbyterian Church took place.

In the past Windsor was renowned for sending out missionaries across the world, including my grandparents. The tide has turned and in recent years, under the theme 'Faith Without Borders', Windsor has provided a welcome to Christians, some of them refugees, from all over the world. I hope that today's diverse and multi-national Windsor congregation will continue to thrive in its new location in Great Victoria Street. As for the building, it has been sold to a theatre company. The original Lyric Theatre had its birth a few doors away in Derryvolgie Avenue.

I watched the last service at Windsor online. Seeing the familiar wooden panelling, the octagonal pulpit and stained-glass windows, I was reminded of the close-knit community of my childhood. We worshipped together in the church, played badminton and bowls and took part in shows in the Lecture Hall, and enjoyed our annual grandstand view of the Twelfth parade. It was a caring community: we called it fellowship. I can still see the families sitting in their pews – Boyds, Baileys, Dundees, Farises, Gibsons, Rankins, Wilsons, Browns, Bamfords, McMorrans, Kellys, and so many more. With Alec McNeilly's huge choir leading the praise, and Hazel McMillan or Peter Russell at the organ, my father's arms would be raised in a benediction. 'The Lord shall preserve thy going out and thy coming in'.

My parents would say, 'God doesn't close one door, but he opens another.' Sure enough, a hundred yards down the road another listed building, the Majestic Cinema, has reopened its doors. Long used as a furniture store and later abandoned and boarded up, our local art deco cinema, where, like young Kenneth Branagh, we watched black and white westerns, has been restored and functions today as… Windsor Baptist Church – but with the MAJESTIC sign still boldly displayed above.

My Windsor Framework

The most recent arrangement between the EU and the UK to resolve the problems in Northern Ireland caused by Brexit has been named the Windsor Framework, after Windsor Castle in England where it was finalised. For a while I considered '*My Windsor Framework*' as a title for this book, since my formative years revolved around our Windsor. Whenever I return to Belfast I am drawn to the area of the church spire, as if by some magnetic force. I see the new shops and restaurants, but, almost as clearly, I see the shops that were there when I was a boy.

Christie's sweetie shop was only a hundred yards away from the manse, next to the Majestic Cinema. Mr Christie was bald and wore a light blue pullover. Mrs Christie wore winged glasses. We were sent there to buy ice cream for dessert – a ripple block with wafers placed in a paper bag. We spent most of our pocket money at Christie's, buying sweets, measured out in quarter pounds from big jars. Clove rock and brandy balls were my favourites.

We suffered the consequences of all those sweeties at the hands of our dentist, Mr Boyle, who worked further down the road in College Gardens. He was bald except for short orange hair at the sides. We knew his scrubbed face with deep pores only too well. Each time we saw him he found three or four cavities, drilled as many holes, and filled our rotten teeth with amalgam, with no anaesthetic to ease the pain.

Sugar wasn't the only addiction that started in Christie's. Sometimes Mum sent us there to buy cigarettes. She didn't smoke much, perhaps ten a week. Mr Christie didn't bat an eyelid when I first asked him for ten Benson & Hedges Silvers, which I later smoked in the attic where I thought that the smell would not descend into the lower regions of the manse.

Mum patronised two shops on the other side of the Lisburn Road. Mr Fleming was a general grocer, also bald, who fetched each item as she read out her list one by one. He brought down Puffed Wheat packets from the highest shelf with the aid of a long stick. Alan Morrison was the greengrocer. He was friendly, with a soft North Antrim accent. His wife was a lovely quiet woman whose birthday was on the same day as Dad's. He always sent her a card. When Mrs Morrison died her husband was inconsolable. I visited the house with Dad. Alan Morrison invited me into the room to pay respects to his dead wife. I couldn't say no. It was the first time I had seen a body lying in a coffin.

Mr Irwin, the chemist, had his shop opposite the manse. He had served in the war and walked with a limp.

He always seemed to be in pain. One Twelfth of July he phoned us to complain that the Union Jack hanging from our manse window had been hoisted upside down, the sign for danger. We quickly corrected our mistake. This experience came in useful to me later when the Union Jack was sometimes wrongly displayed in its line-up with other EU flags at the entrance to EU delegations. Sadly, the Union Flag is no longer present in the line-up of EU member states' flags, to be rightly or wrongly displayed.

A new shop appeared around 1964. The Manchester and Midland sold electric equipment, including record players. Dad bought our first record player, and an LP for each of us – Scottish pipe band music for John, Adam Faith's latest hits for Anne Louise, Chopin's preludes for me, and Mendelsohn's Italian symphony for himself. Dad loved classical music and used to take me to the Ulster Hall for concerts on a Friday evening. The Italian symphony was the first music we heard there together.

Across the road was Percy's bicycle shop, where Dad bought my first bike, a Hercules. I thought it was new but later found out it was an old bike reconstructed with new handlebars. From the beginning of October each year, Percy stocked fireworks. Together with the Farises we diverted all our pocket money during the month to building up a collection of fireworks and rockets for a display supervised by Professor Faris at Hallowe'en.

Next door to Percy's bicycle shop was a small garage owned by Moore and Oliver. One was Catholic and the other Protestant and they had two apprentices, one Catholic and one Protestant. This was where Mum's car, a second-hand blue Ford Anglia, was serviced. John and

I learnt to drive in it, taught by a retired policeman how to avoid all the potholes on the road to Lisburn, and to 'asselerate, for God's sake, asselerate', on the way home. The biggest disappointment and shame in my young life was when I failed my driving test. I passed the second time, and my folks allowed me to drive the Anglia when I went courting.

A girlfriend in 1972 lived across town in North Queen Street, a dangerous area. To reach her at the weekend I had to drive in the dark through the centre of Belfast and cross police and army checkpoints. One Saturday evening, after I had returned safely home, I found my parents both awake. This was unusual. Mum usually stayed up, but Dad never let my movements upset his Saturday sleep. They were relieved to see me alive. There had been incidents all evening across Belfast, one just across the road from us. A gunman had walked into Moore and Oliver's garage and shot dead the Catholic apprentice. At the time, tit-for-tat killings were happening in Belfast every few days. Opposite the church, Stewarts, the new supermarket that had replaced the small grocers' shops, was destroyed in an almighty explosion. This time there was a warning and no one was killed.

It was either Mr Moore or Mr Oliver, I'm not sure which, who came up to me at Dad's funeral and told me that he thought Dad was a great man.

'Your dad went into the home of that young Catholic boy. He met the whole family, who were in an awful state, and he prayed with them, and he managed to take the hate away. It was a wonderful thing that he did.'

Last June, I visited Belfast for a family funeral.

Afterwards I looked in to my old Lisburn Road neighbourhood. Stewarts has been replaced by Tesco. The Manchester and Midland has become an estate agency. A block of flats occupied the spot where Moore and Oliver's garage once stood. I walked down the road to Shaftesbury Square and was having a pizza at a place on Bedford Street when I noticed across the road a big crowd going into the Ulster Hall. Was there something on? I realised that it was a Friday evening, at a quarter to eight. This would be the right time for the Ulster Orchestra. I crossed over and bought one of the last tickets. They played Mendelsohn, not the Italian symphony, but the violin concerto. I looked upwards, the way that footballers sometimes do after they score a goal. *'This one's for you, Dad'.*

Caithness

Returning from Orkney last year we visited Caithness, the most northerly county in Scotland, for the first time. Walking around the old town we saw posters advertising Caithness flagstones that have long been used as pavements in cities throughout Scotland and beyond. So, when our architect in Edinburgh proposed to choose Caithness stone to replace the gravel that surrounds our new house, I liked the idea.

We decided to use the same stone for a new patio halfway along the southern side of the house. There is a place on the path, between two bay windows, that is a perfect sun trap. The idea came to me to carve out an octagon there, extending from the walls of the house into the garden. The architect prepared a detailed design, including some steps. This octagonal patio, paved in Caithness stone, would be an ideal spot for meals al fresco, with family and friends, on the days when Edinburgh weather permits such Mediterranean extravagances.

A few months later I sat down to work on the chapter of this book in which I wrote about my father's sermons. I had been struggling with this for a while, just as Dad had often struggled with his own writing. But boy, could the old man tell a story. We especially enjoyed his children's addresses. How could I recapture today the impression Dad's storytelling made and the lessons he taught us?

It occurred to me that I still had old cassette tapes of Dad's preaching from services once broadcast on the radio. I hadn't listened to them this century and no longer even owned a tape recorder. I ordered a Walkman-like device, which Amazon delivered the next day, and sat down to listen to a service first broadcast on RTE radio from St Johnston in Donegal on Sunday 24 February 1980, a month before Luisa was born.

The cassette had stopped in the middle of the service. I didn't press rewind, in case the new machine would eat up the old brown tape. I just pressed play, and the congregation sprang to life, singing a psalm. Donegal voices in harmony. Winnie McCracken at the organ. I wondered how many of that congregation are alive today.

A woman read a lesson from the New Testament with great gusto and in a lovely accent – a Laggan lilt. It was the story of the man who built his house on stone and the one who built his house on sand.

The voice that followed was even clearer, and still holds power over me, whether I hear it on tape, or in my head. Dad had an engaging speaking voice, with an unmistakable North Antrim accent and intonation. He pronounced 'not' as 'nought', an indicator of his origin in the Route district. He also rolled his Rs, a trick he may have acquired from listening to Scots pulpit orators such as George MacLeod and DP Thompson.

He began the children's address, pausing between each phrase:

What an exciting picture Jesus gives us in those verses. Two men in two houses and then the rain, floods and gales. One house stands up to it, and the other one comes down with a great crash.

GiRRls and boys, let's hope the weather is 'nought' like that when you go to school tomorrow.

Do you know that in some parts of Scotland when it's raining hard, and the children cannot get out to play, they sing this little rhyme?:

> *'Rainy rainy, rattle and stainy*
> *Don't rain on me,*
> *Rain on John O'Groats' house,*
> *Far ayont the sea.'*

Now that's funny, because John O'Groats' house is not far beyond the sea. It's in the north of Scotland, in Caithness, almost in the sea. Maybe you will go there one day and see it for yourselves.

I smiled to myself, as I listened. How did you know, Dad, that I've just visited Caithness for the first time?

But who was this man John O'Groats? We are told that many years ago, in the reign of James IV, there came to Scotland a Dutch man called Jan de Groot. He had eight sons, and by and by they all married and had homes of their own, but once a year, on a certain date, they all came back to see their father and to celebrate the day when he arrived in Scotland.

On one of those yearly visits, unfortunately, these eight sons started quarreling among themselves as to which one should be the boss and sit at the top of the table. Not so nice for the old man, was it? Well, they all turned to him to decide and settle the dispute. And all he said was, 'All right, all right, come back all of you next year and I'll tell you.'

The next year, when they all came back for the anniversary dinner, they found that their father had built a room with eight sides to it, and on each side a door, and in the centre of the room a table with eight sides. So, there was nothing to quarrel over. Each son could walk in by a different door and sit at a different side of the table. All eight of them were equal.

Clever old man, John O'Groats. Mind you, we are not told if that ended the quarrel among the brothers. I do hope so. But d'you know, our Lord Jesus had the same trouble with his twelve disciples. One day he found that several of them had started to quarrel because each wanted to be head disciple. And our Lord was much cleverer and wiser than old John O'Groats. This is what he said to them.

'Whoever wants to be greatest among you must be your servant.'

And to show them what he meant, Jesus took a basin of water and a towel and stood down and washed the sand from his disciples' feet.

Today a new octagon, paved with Caithness stone, has been carved into our Edinburgh garden. When we gather there and talk of times gone by, with friends or as a family, with Paola and our children and grandchildren, perhaps there is also a voice pronouncing a benediction, and invoking the names of the Father, the Son and the Holy Spirit – some sort of invisible glue that binds us all together.

Acknowledgements

Parts of this book were published in an earlier form in a blog entitled 'Closely Related to Chester'. I thank John Faris, Alan Gaston, Carmen Michael, and Dr WD Boyd for their encouraging comments.

Thanks also to Tony Farr, Neil Faris, Paul Malin, Axel Pougin de La Maisonneuve and Malcolm Wood, who provided valuable observations on specific chapters.

My English teacher, the poet Michael Longley, kindly allowed me to quote from his poem and inspired me to write of the conversations with my father, the ones we had and 'those we never had'.

Rev. Ruth Patterson kindly allowed me to reproduce her poem about Cahal Daly.

My wife, Paola Fornari Hanna, has written a beautiful book about her parents and her childhood in Africa, entitled *Leap into the Light*. She encouraged me to write about my own parents and my childhood, and greatly helped with editing this book, correcting as many of my mistakes as she could lay her hands on. The rest belong entirely to me.

Select Bibliography

Bardon, Jonathan, *A Narrow Sea*, Gill, 2019

BBC, *Two Centuries of Irish History*, 1974

Biagini & Mulhall, *The Shaping of Modern Ireland*, Irish Academic Press, 2016

Bresland, *The Backward Glance – C.S. Lewis and Ireland*, 1999

Brown, Robert, *Windsor Presbyterian Church*, 1987

Caldwell, Lucy, *These Days*, Faber, 2022

Carson, Jan, *The Raptures*, Doubleday, 2022

Cervantes, *Don Quixote*, 1605

Craig, Patricia, *The Ulster Anthology*, Blackstaff, 2006

Daly, Cahal B, *The Minding of Planet Earth*, Veritas, 2004

Daly, Cahal B, *Steps on My Pilgrim Journey*, Veritas, 1998

Davey, Ernest, *Religious Experience*, Artis, 2021

Devlin, Bernadette, *The Price of My Soul*, 1969

Fleming, Ian, *Casino Royale*, Jonathan Cape, 1953

Greenberger, Scott S, *The Unexpected President*, Da Capo Press, 2017

Hanna, William D, *Voyages with My Grandfather*, Matador, 2020

Keatinge, Patrick, *A Place among the Nations*, IPA, 1978

Joyce, James, *Portrait of the Artist as a Young Man*, 1916

Joyce, James, *Ulysses*, 1922

Longley, Michael, *Collected Poems*, Jonathan Cape, 2006

MacKay, Susan, *Northern Protestants on Shifting Ground*, Blackstaff, 2021

MacNeice, Louis, *The Strings Are False*, Faber, 2007

Moloney, Ed, *Paisley*, Poolbeg, 2008

Moody & Martin, *The Course of Irish History*, RTE, 1977

O'Brien, Conor Cruise, *Ancestral Voices*, Poolbeg, 1994

O'Brien, Flann, *At Swim-Two-Birds*, Penguin, 1939

O'Toole, Fintan, *We Don't Know Ourselves*, Apollo, 2022

Pagnol, Marcel, *La Gloire de mon Père*, 1957

Rafter, Kevin, *Martin Mansergh – A Biography*, New Island, 2002

Rodgers, WR, *Poems*, The Gallery Press, 1969

Scott, Sir Walter, *Old Mortality*, 1816

Sellar & Yeatman, *1066 and All That*, Methuen, 1930

Smith, Dodie, *101 Dalmatians*, 1956

Sterne, Laurence, *The Life and Opinions of Tristram Shandy, Gentleman*, 1759

Stevenson, Robert Louis, *Edinburgh*, 1878